EXPLORING
SHAKESPEARE
SERIES

MACBETH

educate.ie

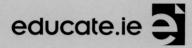

PUBLISHED BY:
Educate.ie
Walsh Educational Books Ltd
Castleisland, Co. Kerry, Ireland
www.educate.ie

ASSOCIATE EDITOR:
Peter Malone

PRODUCTION EDITOR:
Kieran O'Donoghue

DESIGN/ILLUSTRATIONS:
The Design Gang, Tralee

PRINTED AND BOUND BY:
Walsh Colour Print, Castleisland

PHOTOGRAPHS –
Main photographs by Karl Hugh (courtesy of Utah Shakespeare Festival, USA) and Kevin Byrne. See page 240 for full list of actors and productions.
   Other photographs courtesy of Shakespeare Globe Theatre, BigStock, Istock, Stockbyte/Getty.

The author and publisher have made every effort to trace all copyright holders. If any have been overlooked we would be happy to make the necessary arrangements at the first opportunity.

ISBN: 978-1-908507-40-2

Dedication

For my mother, Joan Antoinette

Acknowledgements

I would like to thank my inspiring students and supportive colleagues (past and present) at Yeats College in Waterford. A very special thank you to my wonderful family and friends, and everyone at Educate.ie, especially Peter Malone. Thanks to Elaine Costelloe for her initial feedback.

– Mary Barron

CONTENTS

PREFACE

This edition of Shakespeare's Macbeth has been designed with you, the student, in mind. The text is packed with notes, summaries, character studies and sample essays – in short, everything you need for exam success.

While it is true to say that every word in Macbeth is significant, all of the play's most important quotations have been underlined. This is to draw your attention to those that are most meaningful and will also help you to decide what quotations you need to memorise. When you are doing that, you should try to choose quotations from a range of characters and themes. Choose multifunctional ones when possible. A quotation such as 'Lest our old robes sit easier than our new!' could be used for character questions on Macbeth or Macduff, for stylistic questions on imagery, or for thematic questions, such as a question on 'kingship', for example.

For ease of reference, each act is colour-coded, and the notes include an explanation of each scene, as well as a longer analysis of each act. These notes are presented in a concise, focused way, so you can learn them confident in the knowledge that you can use all the material therein in the exam.

Many scenes have been translated into modern English. Although Shakespeare's language is very eloquent, it is also interesting to see how these words might be spoken today. These scenes are useful for revision and will help you to get to know the text really well, though of course they are not meant to replace the poetry of Shakespeare's own dialogue.

There are detailed character studies here, too. You will have formed your own impressions of the characters by the time you have finished studying the text. Considering your opinions and these notes together will help to give you a well-rounded view of the characters in the play.

All of the important themes in Macbeth are explained thoroughly in the notes. As well as that, there is a comprehensive section on how to answer exam questions, and there are many helpful sample essays for you to emulate in your own writing.

Most important, Macbeth is an astounding play, written by a playwright at the height of his powers, so enjoy the play, and form your own opinions of it.

Mary Bannen

INTRODUCTION

MACBETH, WRITTEN between 1605 and 1606, marks the high point of Shakespeare's dramatic career. There was a real Macbeth in the eleventh century, but Shakespeare's play is almost completely fictional. He uses historical names and places, and some facts, but most of the story is his own invention. In fact, all of Shakespeare's plays were loosely inspired by existing stories, plays or historical events, but he always put a lot of his own thoughts, philosophy and, of course, eloquent language into each and every one.

Macbeth is a play about ambition. All of us can relate to this trait to a degree. And while most people would never go so far as to kill a king to satisfy their ambitions, there are many people who compromise themselves in smaller ways: the person who doesn't tell colleagues about a new promotion because he wants it for himself, for example; or the student who discovers a great new website full of really helpful Leaving Cert material, but keeps it to herself! We can all relate to choosing to do the wrong thing. The division between good and evil is not always a chasm; more often, it may just be a line in the sand.

Macbeth also has a resonance in political life, past and present. We have all seen how 'Power tends to corrupt and absolute power corrupts absolutely.' Think of the dictators of the twentieth century: Hitler, Mussolini and Stalin. These men were obsessed with establishing their rule, because it gave them the power they so ardently desired. Or we could think of Roman emperors such as Nero or Caligula. Like Macbeth, their abominable machinations were all carried out to satisfy their boundless, greedy ambition. More recently, the world has been riven by power-hungry men like Saddam Hussein, Osama bin Laden and Muammar Gaddafi. In Ireland, we have seen how politicians will make promises during election times and then forget about them when elected. Many politicians do not seem to want to be in public office to serve the public; instead they want the power and status that the office brings. As the great philosopher Plato wrote, 'Those who seek power are not worthy of that power.' The very fact that Macbeth wants power so desperately that he will kill for it is the very reason he should not have power at all.

These are just some of the reasons why a play like *Macbeth* continues to be so relevant and applicable to our times and to our own lives. There are many other reasons too, such as the fact that sometimes people do the wrong thing for the right reasons, as Lady Macbeth does. The play also asks if evil is an active choice or a trait that people are born with, and this is also an interesting proposition.

Macbeth is constructed in a very clever way. The Witches' prophecies and the Apparitions are revealed to be treacherous mind tricks, while the tragic denouement is quite brilliant. Certain words and phrases are repeated throughout the play, and the playwright creates suspense, tension and intrigue at every turn. The characters are skilfully developed and utterly realistic. Just as in real life, no one is perfect, but all are very human and thus recognisable. *Macbeth* is a masterpiece indeed. Enjoy it.

THE LIFE AND TIMES OF
WILLIAM
SHAKESPEARE

'He was not of an age, but for all time!'

— BEN JONSON

W ILLIAM SHAKESPEARE was a brilliant and prolific poet and playwright. He was born in Stratford-upon-Avon in 1564, the third child in his family, but the first surviving child after two sisters died in infancy. His father, John, was a glove-maker and a wine merchant. The family's fortunes were mixed. They were wealthy at first, but later John lost much of his fortune and later still regained it again. This may be why Shakespeare is so egalitarian, and it is often the lower-ranking characters, like the Nurse in *Romeo and Juliet* or Nerissa in *The Merchant of Venice*, who steal the show. In *King Lear*, to give another example, the servants show more loyalty to the king than do his own daughters.

Shakespeare, unlike many of his characters (who tended to be rich or royal, or both) lived in the real world. His family endured their share of tragedy, as only five of their eight children survived into adulthood, and then Shakespeare's beloved younger brother, Edmund, died in 1607, when he was just twenty-seven.

We presume that Shakespeare went to grammar school in Stratford, but he did not attend either Oxford or Cambridge, so he was obviously self-taught, which makes his achievements all the more astonishing. Books were not easily available in those days, but it is clear that Shakespeare was incredibly well read and that he went to a lot of effort to educate himself. It is obvious from the breadth and depth of his works that he had a voracious curiosity about the world around him.

Shakespeare married at the young age of eighteen. It is often presumed that, like Romeo and Juliet, everyone in Shakespeare's era married in their teens. In fact, the average marriage age was in the mid-twenties, and the age of consent for a man was twenty-one. Shakespeare, however, married for one of the most obvious of reasons: his bride, Anne Hathaway, was pregnant. She was twenty-six, eight years his senior, so there was quite a significant age gap between them, something that was particularly scandalous at that time. The couple's first daughter, Susanna, was born in 1583, followed by twins, Hamnet and Judith, two years later. Tragically, Shakespeare's son Hamnet died aged just eleven, and this had a profound effect on his writing. It became deeper and darker after his terrible loss. Macduff's moving speech when he learns of the death of his children in Act IV, Scene III of *Macbeth* was undoubtedly inspired by Shakespeare's own loss. 'I must feel it as a man,' he says, echoing the playwright's own experience.

Given that the couple had just three children and that Shakespeare spent most of his adult life in London, many biographers surmise that William and Anne's marriage was not a happy one. Much has been made of the fact that in his will Shakespeare bequeathed Anne his 'second-best bed' and nothing more! This sounds rather unchivalrous, but in fact it was common practice then to leave everything to your children rather than your spouse. And the second-best bed would have been the marital bed; the best one would have been kept for guests. While the evidence, as always, is scant, many would agree that the couple did separate, in deed if not in word. There have been many hypotheses put forward about Shakespeare's relationships with other women (and there have also been unsubstantiated rumours of dalliances with men), but in the end we simply do not know. What we do know is that Shakespeare did return to Stratford to retire, so whatever their changing circumstances, the couple were perhaps in truth happily married. The playwright certainly experienced great passion. His many sonnets often concern themselves with that most universal of themes, love.

Despite the fact that so much of Shakespeare's writing is still extant, we tend to feel we know very little about him, especially in comparison with what we know about more modern writers. He is sometimes viewed as an unreliable charlatan, who bluffed his way through an amazing dramatic career (many volumes have been devoted to the study of lacunae – gaps or missing parts – in his works). Other scholars are convinced that he was a man to whom honour meant everything. What we do know for sure is that Shakespeare was an astute observer of the human condition. His plays indicate that he was a detached spectator, someone on the periphery of society, well placed to judge those around him. He saw the misfortune and cruelty of life – this was an age when unfortunate criminals might be hanged on the street – but rather than losing his humanity, he became a compassionate recorder of what it means to be human. Shakespeare recognised that not many people are truly evil, and few are completely good. Morality is not black and white. There is a huge grey area between good and evil, and it is on this that *Macbeth* and his other great tragedies, *Hamlet*, *King Lear* and *Othello*, focus.

After leaving Stratford-upon-Avon in his early twenties, the life Shakespeare lived must have been colourful. He was drawn to the theatre – most biographers believe that he would have found settled family life no substitute for the dramatic world – and he began his career as an actor. Acting troupes regularly visited Stratford, and may have recruited him there, or he may have followed them to London. His experience as an actor helped him forge a real connection with the audience; he knew what made them laugh and what made them cry. Writing was a natural progression. Now he learned how to create brilliant stories to capture his audiences' attention.

Shakespeare began to make a name for himself as a poet, and, with some powerful personalities such as the Earl of Southampton numbered among his admirers, he quickly grew in stature. Shakespeare's success as a poet gave his name a certain cachet, and drew audiences to the point where his troupe of actors, the Lord Chamberlain's Men, later the King's Men, were easily the most successful of the day. After London's theatres had to shut for some years because of the plague, when they reopened in 1593 there was a void to be filled. Shakespeare was just the playwright to fill it.

Timing and circumstance played their part in contributing to his success, as they often do.

Shakespeare deals with many themes in his plays and poetry: love, hatred, kingship, ambition, mercy, greed, violence, war, filial duty and revenge. All these themes are universal, and so they are always relevant. He portrays his characters in all their human frailty; his heroes are not infallible, and that is why they engage our sympathy.

Shakespeare's plays are classed as the tragedies, the comedies and the histories. The tragedies are full of torment and suffering, whereas the comedies are full of humour and happy timing. Yet every tragedy has at least some comic elements (such as the Porter's scene in *Macbeth*), and every comedy has a little tragedy. All of Shakespeare's heroes have 'fatal flaws', human weaknesses that contribute to their downfall. This makes the characters so very believable, and their tragedy all the more tragic.

Shakespeare regularly presented plays for Queen Elizabeth I's enjoyment. She was not easy to please and would often send specific instructions on the kind of play she wished to see. This would sometimes call for last-minute rewrites and a lot of improvising! Elizabeth ruled England, without ever marrying, for over forty years. For a woman to hold the highest position in the kingdom was an amazing accomplishment at a time when women had no social power and were considered mere possessions of men.

Shakespeare was clearly trying to please the queen when he wrote strong female characters, such as Portia, who saves the day in *The Merchant of Venice*, even though she is obliged to disguise herself as a man. This is all the more remarkable when you remember that, in this period, women weren't actually allowed on stage, so their parts were played by men.

Shakespeare was ahead of his time in his treatment of female characters. While many of his contemporaries polarised women into angels or whores, Shakespeare's female characters are realistic human beings, in all their frailty. No doubt, the reign of such a strong woman as Elizabeth I in his lifetime influenced Shakespeare's view of women.

Elizabeth never married, and she left no heirs. When she died in 1603, England's 'Golden Age', a period when theatre and the arts flourished, ended with her. Her successor, King James I, was a more moderate ruler than Elizabeth, but he was also less devoted to the arts. Shakespeare was still favoured at court, however, and he probably changed the character of Banquo (historically, he was Macbeth's accomplice) to flatter the king, who was reputed to be Banquo's descendant. James also had an obsessive fascination with witches, and this accounts for the supernatural element in *Macbeth*.

Shakespeare wrote many of his greatest works – *King Lear, Othello, Hamlet* and *Macbeth* – between 1600 and 1605. They made Shakespeare famous in his own lifetime and he was able to retire to Stratford-upon-Avon a wealthy man. He continued writing almost to the end of his life, but the passion and ferocity of the great quartet of tragedies was notably absent from his later plays. While his writing continued to be as elegant and insightful as ever, Shakespeare mellowed in his later years, and as a result his later works tended to be more gentle and philosophical. *Macbeth* can be viewed as the work of a younger, angrier man, when the playwright was at the very height of his genius.

It is not just as a writer that Shakespeare excels, but also as a man with the deepest level of human understanding. Shakespeare understood people. He understood the human condition, our triumphs and our failings, the fact that we are capable of the ridiculous, but also the sublime. Many characters in *Macbeth* could, quite feasibly, be based on the major characters of Shakespeare's day. Perhaps Lady Macbeth was based on Anne Boleyn, who manipulated Henry VIII so expertly and yet came to such a terrible end (she was beheaded in 1536), as well as being inspired by her daughter, Elizabeth I. But beyond his brilliant characterisation of the people of his era, perhaps Shakespeare's insight was an innate gift, the kind of transcendent knowing we find in a Van Gogh painting or a Beethoven concerto. Certainly many of the playwright's lines have passed down through the years as gems of wisdom, such as the expression 'be true to yourself', which comes from *Hamlet*: 'To thine own self be true, And it must follow, as the night the day, Thou can'st not then be false to any man.'

Much has been written about William Shakespeare, and if you want to find out more about his life, Bill Bryson's entertaining book, *Shakespeare: The World as Stage*, is well worth a read, as is *In Search of Shakespeare* by Michael Woods, which is very insightful and beautifully illustrated. The film *Elizabeth* (1998), starring Cate Blanchett, gives a great insight into Elizabeth I's life and reign.

ELIZABETHAN THEATRE

THE LAYOUT of the Elizabethan stage was very simple. There were few props, no scenery, and the actors were on view the entire time. The stage, which projected out into the theatre, had a rectangular shape. The theatre itself was a large semicircle. The pit immediately around the stage was not covered with a roof. This was where the groundlings, the poorer members of the audience, stood. Around the perimeter were tiered rows of seats, which were covered against the elements, for the merchant and noble classes, and in the centre, directly facing the stage, was the royal box for the queen and her retinue.

Shakespeare's company put on their productions at the Globe Theatre, built in 1599, until 1608, when they leased the Blackfriar's Theatre, which had the advantage of a full roof. The Lord Chamberlain's Men, who later became the King's Men, included some of the most famous actors of the day. Acting was a hard existence for most, though. They were badly paid and often ill-treated by their audience.

The Elizabethans who came to the theatre were a very different audience from any we might find today. We are saturated with media in the twenty-first century. We have cinema, television, radio, iPads, computers, iPods, and as many books, magazines and newspapers as we could want. Imagine a time when none of these were available, when, if you were very wealthy, you might be lucky enough to own a few books. Most people, however, were illiterate, and they worked long, hard hours with very little respite or entertainment. Even a long church service lasting several hours was a welcome break in those dreary times. Indeed, touring companies brought 'Passion Plays' around the country, where they would act out scenes from the life of Christ on the village green. We would probably find these plays quite heavy going, but in those days people would eagerly queue for hours to see them.

When Shakespeare's audience came to the theatre, they wanted to be entertained with stories. They wanted to hear about the lives of the wealthy and the titled, to learn of exotic countries which they knew they would never see. They

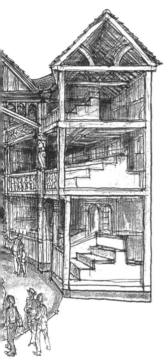

*LEFT: **An artist's impression of London's Globe Theatre in Shakespeare's day, showing a cross-section of the building***

*BELOW: **The Globe Theatre, reconstructed in 1997 and dedicated to the exploration of Shakespeare's work***

most inhumane way. But, on the other hand, they were quite innocent. They believed in ghosts and witches, for example, and were terrified of them. Shakespeare used such fears to grab their attention.

Plays in the Elizabethan era were principally an entertainment, but they could also be vehicles for social or political criticism, just as they often are today. *King Lear* highlights the plight of the poor and the excesses of the rich. *The Merchant of Venice* seems anti-Semitic today, but in its time it was seen as pro-Christian. In *Macbeth*, Shakespeare clearly criticises those who would do anything for power, and there were many in his day.

As you read through *Macbeth* in class and see it in performance on stage or in film, always think of the original audience for whom, after all, it was written. Think of how frightened they would have been by the Witches, and how horrified they would have been by regicide. Imagine their astonishment at scenes such as the cauldron scene, and their amazement at the clever twists in the play's finale. This will help you to understand the brilliance of Shakespeare's drama and give you a unique insight into the play.

You might also like to note that the 1998 film *Shakespeare in Love,* although it is almost wholly fictional, gives a great view of Shakespeare's life in the theatre.

expected drama, intrigue and suspense. A tragedy had to be really tragic; a comedy had to make them laugh heartily. If the audience did not like the play, they would pelt the actors with eggs and rotten fruit in protest. Often, someone would start throwing missiles during the briefest lull in the play, so Shakespeare and other playwrights had to make sure to hold their interest. The audience were incredibly hardened in some respects – they would often have seen dead bodies hanging from the gallows or people being tortured in the

MACBETH

11

SHAKESPEARE'S ENGLISH

YOU MAY find the language used in Shakespeare's plays difficult at first, but as you grow more familiar with the play you will find that it becomes easier to understand. Language is always in a state of flux, always growing and changing. Ten years ago, for example, you might have said, 'I'll look that up on the Internet,' but now you might just say, 'I'll Google it.' Or someone might say, 'I have to do the hoovering,' when what they really mean to do is vacuum the carpet. 'Hoover' is a brand of vacuum cleaner, but, like Google, so many people had Hoovers that it became a common noun and a verb, as well as a product. Another example of how language is constantly changing is that the Oxford English Dictionary added the expression 'D'oh!' to the lexicon in 2002. Because *The Simpsons* is so popular, Homer's catchphrase has become known, and used, the world over.

You can tell a lot about a society from its language. The English spoken in Ireland is known as Hiberno-English, and it has a particular character and poetry. An Irish person might say, 'I'm after doing that already,' an expression that makes no sense to an English person (for whom 'after' means 'behind' or 'later than'), but we know what it means because it comes from the Irish *'tar éis'*. Ireland has traditionally been a very religious country, too, and our greetings make this apparent. We say *'Dia duit'* for hello, and the response is *'Dia is Muire duit.'* These characteristics give the works of writers like John B. Keane and Patrick Kavanagh a particular eloquence, which Irish people are naturally proud of. English was never formally taught in Ireland, until it eventually replaced Irish as our main language, and this accounts for the relative informality of Irish speech. 'I had a right mare of a day,' we might say, to describe a particularly hard day, or a person from the country might be described as a 'culchie'.

If you consider that *Macbeth* was written 400 years ago, it is no wonder that the language is so different from what we use today. What is not so different, however, are people themselves. We use language as a tool for communication. It expresses our practical needs, but also our deeper emotions and desires. Language is our most eloquent form of expression.

The Elizabethans had an incredibly colourful language. Some words are almost onomatopoeic. To 'beslubber' someone, for example, meant to say something bad about them. Even if we are not familiar with the word, 'beslubber' still sounds like an awful thing to do! They also had lots of words for partying and making merry, like 'carousing' and 'capering'. Some words and phrases considered rude then would not be considered at all offensive today. A 'worsted-stocking knave' was a terrible insult. It meant your stockings (men wore white knitted stockings under puffy shorts at one stage) were sagging, and someone could take deep offence at such a remark. On the other hand, 'shit' is considered impolite now, but in Shakespeare's day it was a perfectly acceptable verb and noun.

With Shakespeare, it can be the 'thou's and 'thee's which put us off, as those terms are no longer in common usage. Also, there is a tendency to drop 'e's, as in 'quench'd', 'shriek'd' or 'drugg'd', so the word looks unfamiliar on the page. However, you soon get used to it, and to the characters' tendency to greet each other formally, with their 'Noble sir'

A CAMP NEAR FORRES. ALARUM WITHIN

*Enter Duncan, Malcolm, Donalbain, Lennox, with
Attendants, meeting a bleeding Sergeant*

Duncan
What bloody man is that? He can report,
As seemeth by his plight, of the revolt
The newest state.

Malcolm
This is the sergeant
Who like a good and hardy soldier fought   5
'Gainst my captivity. Hail, brave friend!
Say to the King the knowledge of the broil
As thou didst leave it.

Sergeant
Doubtful it stood,
As two spent swimmers that do cling together   10
And choke their art. The merciless Macdonwald[3] –
Worthy to be a rebel, for to that
The multiplying villainies of nature
Do swarm upon him – from the Western Isles
Of kerns and gallowglasses[4] is supplied;   15
And Fortune, on his damned quarrel smiling,
Show'd like a rebel's whore. But all's too weak;
For brave Macbeth – well he deserves that name –
Disdaining Fortune, with his brandish'd steel,
Which smok'd with bloody execution,   20
Like Valour's minion[5] carved out his passage
Till he faced the slave,
Which ne'er shook hands, nor bade farewell to him,
Till he unseam'd him from the nave to the chaps,
And fix'd his head upon our battlements.   25

Duncan
O valiant cousin! Worthy gentleman!

Sergeant
As whence the sun 'gins his reflection
Shipwrecking storms and direful thunders break,
So from that spring whence comfort seem'd to come
Discomfort swells. Mark, King of Scotland, mark!   30

[3] *Macdonwald (the Thane of Cawdor)
is a traitor to Scotland*

[4] *Kerns and gallowglasses were
two ranks of soldiers*

[5] *A servant of Valour, i.e. he is brave*

No sooner justice had, with valour arm'd,
Compell'd these skipping kerns to trust their heels,
But the Norweyan[6] lord, surveying vantage,
With furbish'd arms and new supplies of men,
Began a fresh assault.   35

Duncan   Dismay'd not this
Our captains, Macbeth and Banquo?

Sergeant   Yes,
As sparrows eagles, or the hare the lion.
If I say sooth, I must report they were   40
As cannons overcharged with double cracks,
So they doubly redoubled strokes upon the foe.
Except they meant to bathe in reeking wounds,
Or memorise another Golgotha,[7]
I cannot tell –   45
But I am faint; my gashes cry for help.

Duncan   So well thy words become thee as thy wounds;
They smack of honour both. Go, get him surgeons.

Exit Sergeant, attended

Who comes here?

Enter Ross and Angus

Malcolm   The worthy Thane[8] of Ross.   50

Lennox   What a haste looks through his eyes! So should he look
That seems to speak things strange.

Ross   God save the King!

Duncan   Whence camest thou, worthy Thane?

Ross   From Fife, great King,   55
Where the Norweyan banners flout the sky

[6] *Norweyian*

[7] *Golgotha is the place where Christ was crucified*

[8] *A thane is a high-ranking Scottish nobleman*

And fan our people cold.
Norway himself, with terrible numbers,
Assisted by that most disloyal traitor
The Thane of Cawdor, began a dismal conflict, 60
Till that Bellona's bridegroom,[9] lapp'd in proof,
Confronted him with self-comparisons,
Point against point, rebellious arm 'gainst arm,
Curbing his lavish spirit; and, to conclude,
The victory fell on us. 65

Duncan   Great happiness!

Ross   That now
Sweno, the Norways' king, craves composition;
Nor would we deign him burial of his men
Till he disbursed, at Saint Colmes Inch, 70
Ten thousand dollars[10] to our general use.

Duncan   No more that Thane of Cawdor shall deceive
Our bosom interest. Go pronounce his present death,
And with his former title greet Macbeth.

Ross   I'll see it done. 75

Duncan   What he hath lost, noble Macbeth hath won.

Exit

[9] *Bellona was the ancient Roman goddess of war, so if Macbeth is her 'husband' he also is a god of war*

[10] *This is anachronistic; there were no dollars in Macbeth's day. 'Dollar' here probably means gold coins*

THIS IS FULL of violent and bloody action. Blood is mentioned in the very first line: **What bloody man is that?** We are in the aftermath of a fierce battle. The ground is strewn with dead bodies and body parts. Like so many of the images in *Macbeth*, the scene is hideously violent. King Duncan is talking to his soldiers about Scotland's victory in battle. As in the previous scene, one name stands out: Macbeth. The bleeding Sergeant tells King Duncan about this fierce warrior's ferocious progress in the battle. He slit a man open from his navel to his jaws: **unseam'd him from the nave to the chaps.** We are given an awe-inspiring vision of Macbeth slicing his way through the battle throng: he carved out his passage. Yet we still haven't seen Macbeth. The playwright increases the suspense, as well as our desire to meet this man.

We also learn that Macdonwald, Thane of Cawdor, is a traitor and has betrayed his country by helping the enemy, Sweno of Norway. Duncan plans to execute Cawdor for his treachery and award his title and lands to Macbeth. **No more that Thane of Cawdor shall deceive / Our bosom interest. Go pronounce his present death, / And with his former title greet Macbeth.** The significance of Macbeth's being presented with the Thane of Cawdor's title will be revealed in the next scene.

Shakespeare cleverly whets the audience's appetite, building this whole scene around Macbeth, though the man himself is not present. Now we expect a great hero to make his entrance.

KEY **POINTS**

- *Macbeth is clearly a brave, ferocious warrior. He has killed many of the Norwegian soldiers single-handedly.*

- *This is obviously the battle mentioned by the Witches. They also spoke about meeting Macbeth after the battle, and we await this encounter with growing anticipation.*

- *The Thane of Cawdor has betrayed Duncan and will be punished by death. Macbeth is to be given his title, and thus his lands and wealth. But will he also assume the mantle of traitor?*

A HEATH NEAR FORRES. THUNDER

Enter the three Witches

First Witch	Where hast thou been, sister?
Second Witch	Killing swine.
Third Witch	Sister, where thou?
First Witch	A sailor's wife had chestnuts in her lap,

And mounch'd, and mounch'd, and mounch'd. 'Give   5
    me,' quoth I.
'Aroint[11] thee, witch!' the rump-fed ronyon[12] cries.
Her husband's to Aleppo[13] gone, master o' the Tiger;[14]
But in a sieve I'll thither sail,
And, like a rat without a tail,
I'll do, I'll do, and I'll do.   10

Second Witch	I'll give thee a wind.
First Witch	Thou'rt kind.
Third Witch	And I another.
First Witch	I myself have all the other,

And the very ports they blow,   15
All the quarters that they know
I' the shipman's card.
I will drain him dry as hay:
Sleep shall neither night nor day
Hang upon his penthouse lid;   20
He shall live a man forbid.
Weary se'nnights nine times nine
Shall he dwindle, peak, and pine;
Though his bark cannot be lost,
Yet it shall be tempest-toss'd.   25
Look what I have.

Second Witch	Show me, show me.

11 Get lost!   12 The fat slut
13 An ancient city in Syria   14 A river in Africa

The Witch is going to deprive the woman's husband of sleep so that he will go mad and lose control of his ship. This establishes sleep as essential to people's well-being, a fact that is emphasised later

ACT 1 SCENE III

First Witch	Here I have a pilot's thumb,
	Wreck'd as homeward he did come.
	[Drum within]

Third Witch A drum, a drum! 30
Macbeth doth come.

All The weird sisters, hand in hand,
Posters of the sea and land,
Thus do go about, about;
Thrice to thine, and thrice to mine, 35
And thrice again, to make up nine.
Peace! The charm's wound up.

Enter Macbeth and Banquo

Macbeth So foul and fair a day I have not seen.

Banquo How far is't call'd to Forres? What are these
So wither'd and so wild in their attire, 40
That look not like the inhabitants o' the earth,
And yet are on't? Live you? or are you aught
That man may question? You seem to understand me,
By each at once her choppy finger laying
Upon her skinny lips. You should be women, 45
And yet your beards forbid me to interpret
That you are so.

Macbeth Speak, if you can. What are you?

First Witch All hail, Macbeth! hail to thee, Thane of Glamis!

Second Witch All hail, Macbeth! hail to thee, Thane of Cawdor! 50

Third Witch All hail, Macbeth, that shalt be King hereafter!

Banquo Good sir, why do you start, and seem to fear
Things that do sound so fair? *[To the Witches]* I' the
name of truth,

Are ye fantastical or that indeed
Which outwardly ye show? My noble partner   55
You greet with present grace and great prediction
Of noble having and of royal hope,
That he seems rapt withal. To me you speak not.
If you can look into the seeds of time,
And say which grain will grow and which will not,   60
Speak then to me, who neither beg nor fear
Your favours nor your hate.

First Witch   Hail!

Second Witch   Hail!

Third Witch   Hail!   65

First Witch   Lesser than Macbeth, and greater.

Second Witch   Not so happy, yet much happier.

Third Witch   Thou shalt get kings, though thou be none.
So all hail, Macbeth and Banquo!

First Witch   Banquo and Macbeth, all hail!   70

Macbeth   Stay, you imperfect speakers, tell me more.
By Sinel's[15] death I know I am Thane of Glamis;
But how of Cawdor? The Thane of Cawdor lives,
A prosperous gentleman; and to be King
Stands not within the prospect of belief,   75
No more than to be Cawdor. Say from whence
You owe this strange intelligence, or why
Upon this blasted heath you stop our way
With such prophetic greeting. Speak, I charge you.

Witches vanish

Banquo   The earth hath bubbles, as the water has,   80
And these are of them. Whither are they vanish'd?

[15] *Macbeth's late father*

MACBETH

25

| Macbeth | Into the air, and what seem'd corporal melted |
| | As breath into the wind. Would they had stay'd! |

Banquo	Were such things here as we do speak about?
	Or have we eaten on the insane root
	That takes the reason prisoner?

85

| Macbeth | Your children shall be kings. |

| Banquo | You shall be King. |

| Macbeth | And Thane of Cawdor too. Went it not so? |

| Banquo | To the selfsame tune and words. Who's here? |

90

Enter Ross and Angus

Ross	The King hath happily received, Macbeth,
	The news of thy success; and when he reads
	Thy personal venture in the rebels' fight,
	His wonders and his praises do contend
	Which should be thine or his. Silenced with that,
	In viewing o'er the rest o' the selfsame day,
	He finds thee in the stout Norweyan ranks,
	Nothing afeard of what thyself didst make,
	Strange images of death. As thick as hail
	Came post with post, and every one did bear
	Thy praises in his kingdom's great defence,
	And pour'd them down before him.

95

100

Angus	We are sent
	To give thee, from our royal master, thanks;
	Only to herald thee into his sight,
	Not pay thee.

105

Ross	And for an earnest of a greater honour,
	He bade me, from him, call thee Thane of Cawdor.
	In which addition, hail, most worthy Thane!
	For it is thine.

110

Banquo	*[Aside*[16]*]* What, can the devil speak true?
Macbeth	The Thane of Cawdor lives. Why do you dress me In borrow'd robes?
Angus	Who was the Thane lives yet, But under heavy judgement bears that life Which he deserves to lose. Whether he was combined With those of Norway, or did line the rebel With hidden help and vantage, or that with both He labour'd in his country's wreck, I know not; But treason's capital,[17] confess'd and proved, Have overthrown him.

Macbeth	*[Aside]* Glamis, and Thane of Cawdor!
	The greatest is behind.[18] *[To Ross and Angus]* Thanks for
	    your pains.
	[Aside to Banquo] Do you not hope your children shall
	    be kings,
	When those that gave the Thane of Cawdor to me
	Promised no less to them?

Banquo	*[Aside to Macbeth]* That, trusted home, Might yet enkindle you unto the crown, Besides the Thane of Cawdor. But 'tis strange; And oftentimes, to win us to our harm, The instruments of darkness tell us truths, Win us with honest trifles, to betray 's In deepest consequence – Cousins, a word, I pray you.
Macbeth	*[Aside]* Two truths are told, As happy prologues to the swelling act Of the imperial theme – I thank you, gentlemen. *[Aside]* This supernatural soliciting Cannot be ill, cannot be good. If ill, Why hath it given me earnest of success, Commencing in a truth? I am Thane of Cawdor. If good, why do I yield to that suggestion

Line numbers: 115, 120, 125, 130, 135, 140

[16] A few words spoken privately

[17] He was paid for betraying the king

[18] The 'greatest' part of the Witches' prophecy, i.e. becoming king, is yet to come

Macbeth admits that murderous thoughts are already present in his mind. His own capacity for evil frightens him. It makes his hair stand on end and his heart pound, because it is such an unnatural desire, and he knows it

Whose horrid image doth unfix my hair
And make my seated heart knock at my ribs,
Against the use of nature? Present fears   145
Are less than horrible imaginings:
My thought, whose murder yet is but fantastical,
Shakes so my single state of man that function
Is smother'd in surmise, and nothing is
But what is not.   150

Banquo   Look, how our partner's rapt.

Macbeth   *[Aside]* If chance will have me King, why, chance may
           crown me
Without my stir.

Banquo   New honours come upon him,
Like our strange garments, cleave not to their mould   155
But with the aid of use.

Macbeth   *[Aside]* Come what come may,
Time and the hour runs through the roughest day.

Banquo   Worthy Macbeth, we stay upon your leisure.

Macbeth   Give me your favour; my dull brain was wrought   160
With things forgotten. Kind gentlemen, your pains
Are register'd[19] where every day I turn
The leaf[20] to read them. Let us toward the King.
[To Banquo] Think upon what hath chanced, and at
           more time,
The interim having weigh'd it, let us speak   165
Our free hearts each to other.

Banquo   Very gladly.

Macbeth   Till then, enough. Come, friends.

Exit

Macbeth is clearly trying to emulate Duncan's regal way of expressing himself. This speech is very similar to Duncan's 'Even now the sin of my ingratitude weighs heavily upon me'

[19] *Recorded*
[20] *Page*

THIS IS A CRUCIAL scene. First, we discover that the weird sisters have been up to no good. They punished a sailor's wife for not sharing her chestnuts by depriving her husband of sleep so that he will lose concentration and drown. This tells us that the Witches are creatures not only devoid of conscience but who actually revel in their evil ways.

We finally meet Macbeth, and the first words he speaks in the play echo the very words used by the Witches: *So foul and fair a day I have not seen*. Macbeth is accompanied by his closest friend and comrade in battle, Banquo, whose remarks on the Witches' strange appearance – *What are these / So wither'd and so wild in their attire, / That look not like the inhabitants o' the earth, / And yet are on't?* – evoke images of weird and disturbing creatures. *You should be women, / And yet your beards forbid me to interpret / That you are so.*

(In Shakespeare's time, female roles were played by boys or young men. Normally, they had to wear lots of make-up to appear feminine, but playing the Witches was relatively easy, as they got to grow their beards instead of shaving every day. So scrawny men, dressed as women, would look just as Banquo described.)

The Witches call Macbeth Thane of Glamis, which he is. But then they add: *All hail, Macbeth! hail to thee, Thane of Cawdor … All hail, Macbeth, that shalt be King hereafter!*

(Remember, the audience already knows that Duncan is soon to make Macbeth Thane of Cawdor. This is called dramatic irony, when the audience is aware of something of which the characters are not.)

And oftentimes, to win us to our harm, The instruments of darkness tell us truths

– BANQUO

Macbeth literally jumps at this news, a fact Banquo perceptively notes: *why do you start, and seem to fear / Things that do sound so fair?* Macbeth's reaction shows us that he is ambitious, a trait that was considered highly dangerous in Shakespeare's day. The Witches' words have clearly touched a raw nerve.

Banquo seems a more balanced personality. The Witches say that he is lesser than Macbeth but also greater. He is lesser in that he is of a lower rank. However, he is greater because he does not have the same degree of ambition as Macbeth. Even so, he is also curious about what the Witches have said: *Speak then to me, who neither beg nor fear / Your favours nor your hate.* The Witches respond by telling Banquo that his issue (his descendants) will be kings: *Thou shalt get kings, though thou be none.* Banquo has a son, while Macbeth has no children. Suddenly, in the midst of this intrigue, the Witches ignore Macbeth's appeal for more information, and vanish into thin air.

When Ross arrives with the news that Macbeth is to be made Thane of Cawdor, both men are astonished, given what has just transpired: *What, can the devil speak true?* Banquo shrewdly cautions Macbeth against paying too much heed to the agents of evil: *And oftentimes, to win us to our harm, / The instruments of darkness tell us truths, / Win us with honest trifles, to betray 's / In deepest consequence.* He tells Macbeth that the Witches may be using their knowledge of one event to deceive him into thinking that everything they predict will come true.

But Banquo's sage advice is not heeded. In an aside, Macbeth reveals that he has already contemplated murdering

Duncan. This is a shocking volte-face. The audience has been seduced into believing that Macbeth is a hero. Now we discover a more sinister side to his character. This is a moment of discovery for Macbeth, too:

> *why do I yield to that suggestion*
> *Whose horrid image doth unfix my hair*
> *And make my seated heart knock at my ribs,*
> *Against the use of nature? Present fears*
> *Are less than horrible imaginings:*
> *My thought, whose murder yet is but fantastical,*
> *Shakes so my single state of man that function*
> *Is smother'd in surmise, and nothing is*
> *But what is not.*

Macbeth is frightened by his own thoughts. He is facing an enormous internal struggle, with the characteristics of good and evil battling within his soul. It is also evident that, while Macbeth may be physically strong, he is emotionally weak. He is, indeed, fatally flawed.

KEY **POINTS**

- *The Witches can predict the future and their prophecy is the catalyst for Macbeth's tragic downfall.*

- *Banquo is more balanced and pragmatic than Macbeth.*

- *Macbeth has been sublimating his ambitious tendencies, but his encounter with the Witches is enough to set a tragic chain of events in motion.*

- *The theme of ambition and the theme of good versus evil are both evident in this scene.*

FORRES. THE PALACE

Flourish. Enter Duncan, Malcolm, Donalbain, Lennox, and Attendants

Duncan   Is execution done on Cawdor? Are not
Those in commission yet return'd?

Malcolm   My liege,
They are not yet come back. But I have spoke
With one that saw him die; who did report   5
That very frankly he confess'd his treasons,
Implored your Highness' pardon, and set forth
A deep repentance. Nothing in his life
Became him like the leaving it;[21] he died
As one that had been studied in his death,   10
To throw away the dearest thing he owed
As 'twere a careless trifle.

Duncan   There's no art
To find the mind's construction in the face:
He was a gentleman on whom I built   15
An absolute trust.

Enter Macbeth, Banquo, Ross, and Angus

O worthiest cousin!
The sin of my ingratitude even now
Was heavy on me. Thou art so far before,
That swiftest wing of recompense is slow   20
To overtake thee. Would thou hadst less deserved,
That the proportion both of thanks and payment
Might have been mine! Only I have left to say,
More is thy due than more than all can pay.

Macbeth   The service and the loyalty 1 owe,   25
In doing it, pays itself. Your Highness' part
Is to receive our duties; and our duties

[21] *He died better than he lived. Though a traitor in life, he begged Duncan's forgiveness before his death*

Are to your throne and state, children and servants,
Which do but what they should, by doing everything
Safe toward your love and honour.   30

Duncan   Welcome hither.
I have begun to plant thee, and will labour
To make thee full of growing. Noble Banquo,
That hast no less deserved, nor must be known
No less to have done so; let me infold thee   35
And hold thee to my heart.

Banquo   There if I grow,
The harvest is your own.

Duncan   My plenteous joys,
Wanton in fullness, seek to hide themselves   40
In drops of sorrow. Sons, kinsmen, thanes,
And you whose places are the nearest, know
We will establish our estate[22] upon
Our eldest, Malcolm, whom we name hereafter
The Prince of Cumberland; which honour must   45
Not unaccompanied invest him only,
But signs of nobleness, like stars, shall shine
On all deservers. From hence to Inverness,
And bind us further to you.

Macbeth   The rest is labour, which is not used for you.   50
I'll be myself the harbinger,[23] and make joyful
The hearing of my wife with your approach;
So humbly take my leave.

Duncan   My worthy Cawdor!

Macbeth   [Aside] The Prince of Cumberland! That is a step   55
On which I must fall down, or else o'erleap,
For in my way it lies. Stars, hide your fires;
Let not light see my black and deep desires.
The eye wink at the hand; yet let that be
Which the eye fears, when it is done, to see.   60

[22] Duncan chooses his son, Malcolm, as his successor. Not Macbeth

[23] Messenger

Exit Macbeth

Duncan True, worthy Banquo! He is full so valiant,
And in his commendations I am fed;
It is a banquet to me. Let's after him,
Whose care is gone before to bid us welcome.
It is a peerless kinsman.   65

Flourish. Exit

THIS SHORT SCENE shows us what a fine king Duncan is. Not only is he decisive when he needs to be (ordering the death of the Thane of Cawdor, for example: *Is execution done on Cawdor?*), he is also humble and appreciative. He thanks both Macbeth and Banquo in a heartfelt way and promises them both that they will be richly rewarded for having done their loyal duty to Scotland: *I have begun to plant thee, and will labour / To make thee full of growing.* Duncan also says he will visit Macbeth in his castle at Inverness, which is a tremendous honour. Duncan does not have to thank his thanes so effusively, but it is clear he genuinely appreciates their loyal service.

If Duncan were a bad king, we might understand why Macbeth would want to depose him. If Duncan were an incompetent leader or a bad person, we would not completely condemn Macbeth for his desire to usurp him. However, when Duncan is such a good man, there can be no excuse to justify hurting him. Duncan might be seen as too trusting by a modern audience, but, as he explains, there is no way to tell a person's true personality by their appearance: *There's no art / To find the mind's construction in the face.* (This remark also ties in with the theme of appearance versus reality.)

Macbeth's hypocrisy is quite astounding. He owes Duncan great loyalty, as a thane, a kinsman (Macbeth is Duncan's first cousin), and as a soldier, but his real ambitions are very different. He masks his true feelings with these convincing words:

> *The service and the loyalty I owe,*
> *In doing it, pays itself. Your Highness' part*

Is to receive our duties; and our duties
Are to your throne and state, children and servants,
Which do but what they should, by doing everything
Safe toward your love and honour.

Is it any surprise that Duncan believes him? After all, Macbeth has almost single-handedly defeated Norway in violent battle. He has risked his life for Scotland and the Scottish king. Who would suspect that he did all this despite secretly coveting Duncan's crown?

A key event in this scene is that Duncan names Malcolm as his heir. This seems to surprise Macbeth, although it seems natural that the king would choose his son as his heir. However, as Duncan clearly has the power to choose his successor, perhaps Macbeth was not being as far-fetched as we might first think. In any case, he clearly thought that this was how the Witches' prophecy would come true, that the kingship would be handed to him as effortlessly as the Thanedom of Cawdor was.

Macbeth makes a quick exit, saying that he wishes to delight his wife with the news of Duncan's imminent arrival.

We will establish our estate upon
Our eldest, Malcolm, whom we name hereafter
The Prince of Cumberland

– DUNCAN

In an aside, Macbeth refers once more to his nefarious thoughts, which he wants to remain hidden and not brought into the 'light'; that is, revealed to the world:

> **Stars, hide your fires;**
> **Let not light see my black and deep desires.**
> **The eye wink at the hand; yet let that be**
> **Which the eye fears, when it is done, to see.**

Macbeth is beginning to lose the self-discipline that everyone needs to keep powerful emotions in check. The playwright uses images of day and night to highlight this struggle between good and evil. Light represents good, while darkness represents evil. (In fact, more crimes are committed at night than during the day, so this image is more realistic than it might at first appear.) Yet what is not clear at this point, and perhaps we will never quite understand, is why Macbeth is so ambitious to begin with and why he so badly wants to have power.

Just four scenes into the play, it is evident that Macbeth is as complicated and perplexing as Duncan is guileless and true.

KEY **POINTS**

- *Duncan is an exemplary king, and this establishes the theme of kingship.*

- *Macbeth's ambition has been ignited by the Witches, and he seems powerless faced with his own desires.*

- *Night and day, darkness and light, are used to symbolise good and evil.*

- *The theme of appearance versus reality is also apparent. Duncan was misled by Cawdor's outward show of loyalty and continues to be misled by Macbeth.*

- *Macbeth's dark desires are gaining in momentum after just two scenes. This does not bode well for the future.*

INVERNESS. MACBETH'S CASTLE

Enter Lady Macbeth, reading a letter

Lady Macbeth 'They met me in the day of success, and I have learn'd by
the perfect'st report they have more in them than
mortal knowledge. When I burn'd in desire to question
them further, they made themselves air, into which they
vanish'd. Whiles I stood rapt in the wonder of it, came   5
missives from the King, who all-hailed me "Thane of
Cawdor"; by which title, before, these weird sisters
saluted me and referr'd me to the coming on of time with
"Hail, King that shalt be!" This have I thought good to
deliver thee, my dearest partner of greatness, that thou   10
mightst not lose the dues of rejoicing, by being
ignorant of what greatness is promised thee. Lay it to thy
heart, and farewell.'

Glamis thou art, and Cawdor, and shalt be
What thou art promis'd. Yet do I fear thy nature.   15
It is too full o' the milk of human kindness
To catch the nearest way. Thou wouldst be great,
Art not without ambition, but without
The illness should attend it. What thou wouldst highly,
That wouldst thou holily; wouldst not play false,   20
And yet wouldst wrongly win. Thou'ldst have,
    great Glamis,[24]
That which cries, 'Thus thou must do, if thou have it';
And that which rather thou dost fear to do
Than wishest should be undone. Hie thee hither,
That I may pour my spirits in thine ear,   25
And chastise with the valour of my tongue
All that impedes thee from the golden round,[25]
Which fate and metaphysical[26] aid doth seem
To have thee crown'd withal.

Enter a Messenger

What is your tidings?   30

[24] *Macbeth*

[25] *The crown*
[26] *Supernatural, i.e. the Witches*

Messenger   The King comes here tonight.

Lady Macbeth   Thou'rt mad to say it!
Is not thy master with him? who, were't so,
Would have inform'd for preparation.

Messenger   So please you, it is true; our Thane is coming.   35
One of my fellows had the speed of him,
Who, almost dead for breath, had scarcely more
Than would make up his message.

Lady Macbeth   Give him tending;
He brings great news.   40

Exit Messenger

The raven[27] himself is hoarse
That croaks the fatal entrance of Duncan
Under my battlements.[28] Come, you spirits
That tend on mortal thoughts, unsex me here
And fill me from the crown to the toe top-full   45
Of direst cruelty! Make thick my blood,
Stop up the access and passage to remorse,
That no compunctious[29] visitings of nature
Shake my fell purpose nor keep peace between
The effect and it! Come to my woman's breasts,   50
And take my milk for gall,[30] you murdering ministers,
Wherever in your sightless substances
You wait on nature's mischief! Come, thick night,
And pall thee in the dunnest[31] smoke of hell
That my keen knife see not the wound it makes   55
Nor Heaven peep through the blanket of the dark
To cry, 'Hold, hold!'

Enter Macbeth

Great Glamis! Worthy Cawdor!
Greater than both, by the all-hail hereafter!
Thy letters have transported me beyond   60

[27] *The raven is a bird which symbolises death*

[28] *The parapet on top of a castle, with regular spaces for shooting arrows through*

[29] *Feelings of guilt*

[30] *Bile or poison*

[31] *Thickest*

Lady Macbeth has already decided that Duncan will die in her home. This is a chilling speech, particularly for the original audience, who thought ravens a symbol for the devil as well as death

This ignorant present, and I feel now
The future in the instant.

Macbeth My dearest love,
Duncan comes here tonight.

Lady Macbeth And when goes hence?   65

Macbeth Tomorrow, as he purposes.

Lady Macbeth O, never
Shall sun that morrow see!
Your face, my Thane, is as a book where men
May read strange matters. To beguile[32] the time,   70
Look like the time; bear welcome in your eye,
Your hand, your tongue; look like the innocent flower,
But be the serpent[33] under it. He that's coming
Must be provided for; and you shall put
This night's great business into my dispatch,[34]   75
Which shall to all our nights and days to come
Give solely sovereign sway and masterdom.[35]

Macbeth We will speak further.

Lady Macbeth Only look up clear;
To alter favour ever is to fear.   80
Leave all the rest to me.

Exit

[32] *Enchant, or cast a spell on*

[33] *Snake (which is also a symbol for the devil)*

[34] *Into her hands, i.e. make it her responsibility*

[35] *It is the only thing that they will focus on*

WE ARE INTRODUCED to Lady Macbeth for the first time, and on the stage, as in real life, first impressions count. Lady Macbeth is reading a letter Macbeth has written to her, telling her about the Witches' prophecy. The tone of the letter is not just affectionate; it expresses the deep bond that exists between them: *This have I thought good to deliver thee, my dearest partner of greatness, that thou mightst not lose the dues of rejoicing, by being ignorant of what greatness is promised thee. Lay it to thy heart* … Lady Macbeth is not a typical wife of the time. She is not her husband's powerless possession but his equal partner. He cares a great deal for her, and his eagerness to write to her is quite touching.

It might seem strange that Macbeth writes to his wife, given that he appears in her presence only moments later, but the letter is an important dramatic device. Just as the

> ## The raven himself is hoarse
> ## That croaks the fatal entrance of Duncan
> ## Under my battlements
>
> *– LADY MACBETH*

Witches provided the catalyst for Macbeth's thoughts to turn to evil, this letter acts as a catalyst for his wife. Lady Macbeth's reaction to the letter is immediate and unequivocal: she resolves to play her part in ensuring Macbeth will become king. In fact, she worries that Macbeth is too good a person to commit murder: *too full o' the milk of human kindness / To catch the nearest way.* We have already seen that Macbeth is capable of great actions. His conduct in battle

shows just how great he can be. His wife, however, knows he has good in his heart, but she is sure she can convince him to ignore his scruples and do what he must in order to achieve his desires: *Hie thee hither, / That I may pour my spirits in thine ear, / And chastise with the valour of my tongue / All that impedes thee from the golden round…*

Lady Macbeth is blatant about murdering Duncan. When a messenger informs her of the king's visit, she quickly resolves to kill him: *The raven himself is hoarse / That croaks the fatal entrance of Duncan / Under my battlements.* Macbeth was preoccupied with his dark thoughts, but his wife explicitly refers to action – murderous action. Her language is startling and grotesque:

Come, thick night,

> *And pall thee in the dunnest smoke of hell*
> *That my keen knife see not the wound it makes*
> *Nor Heaven peep through the blanket of the dark*
> *To cry, 'Hold, hold!'*

Yet she also wishes for darkness, so that she does not have to see the truth of what she is doing. This is the first suggestion that Lady Macbeth is not as evil as she initially appears. It also echoes her husband's wish for darkness. This is a further indication of the synchronicity between them.

It is notable that Lady Macbeth asks the forces of darkness for help, and, interestingly, she also asks for her femininity to be suppressed so she can carry out the murder: *Come, you spirits / That tend on mortal thoughts, unsex me here / And fill me from the crown to the toe top-full / Of direst cruelty!* These dark spirits may be not the forces of evil but the Witches themselves, who feed on human thoughts and desires. Lady Macbeth implores the Witches to make her evil, to make her more masculine, to make her cruel.

When Macbeth arrives, he calls his wife his *dearest love*. The fact that Macbeth and Lady Macbeth are equals is really quite exceptional. No doubt the couple have grown close because both are complicit in Macbeth's ambitions. Macbeth confides in his wife, and it is clear that he has not only her wholehearted support, but her utter zeal and determination. His gentle, loving words contrast with much of the language of the play, which is violent and unsettling for the most part.

Macbeth tells his wife that Duncan will stay the night at their castle. This is an extraordinary honour, but the couple also see it is an opportunity, probably the only chance they will ever have of murdering the king and getting away with it. 'Act in haste, repent at leisure,' is an old saying with which Shakespeare would have been familiar. In other words, if you act too hastily, without properly thinking things through, you will almost inevitably do something that you will later come to regret. This is another truism to be found in *Macbeth*.

In the meantime, Lady Macbeth counsels her husband to appear innocent: *look like the innocent flower, / But be the serpent under it.* This is another example of the theme of appearance versus reality. Perhaps Shakespeare is also suggesting that women are better at subterfuge than men.

The scene concludes with an important line from Lady Macbeth: *Leave all the rest to me.* Her words increase the ever-present sense of foreboding running through the play. Macbeth himself may vacillate between good and evil, but his wife has decided what they are going to do. She is the stronger individual, and it is she who will ultimately decide Duncan's fate.

KEY **POINTS**

- *Macbeth and his wife have a deep bond. She will clearly do anything for him, and he trusts in her completely.*

- *Feminine characteristics are seen as an obstacle to evil. One must become masculine in order to commit evil deeds. This raises interesting points about gender and crime.*

- *The theme of appearance versus reality is apparent throughout this scene.*

BEFORE MACBETH'S CASTLE. HAUTBOYS[36] **AND TORCHES**

[36] Archaic word for 'oboe', a wind instrument

Enter Duncan, Malcolm, Donalbain, Banquo, Lennox, Macduff, Ross, Angus, and Attendant

Duncan
This castle hath a pleasant seat; the air
Nimbly and sweetly recommends itself
Unto our gentle senses.

Banquo
This guest of summer,
The temple-haunting martlet,[37] does approve   5
By his loved mansionry[38] that the heaven's breath
Smells wooingly here. No jutty,[39] frieze,[40]
Buttress,[41] nor coign[42] of vantage, but this bird
Hath made his pendant[43] bed and procreant cradle;[44]
Where they most breed and haunt, I have observed   10
The air is delicate.

Enter Lady Macbeth

Duncan
See, see, our honour'd hostess!
The love that follows us sometime is our trouble,
Which still we thank as love. Herein I teach you
How you shall bid God 'ield us for your pains,   15
And thank us for your trouble.

Lady Macbeth
All our service
In every point twice done, and then done double,
Were poor and single business to contend
Against those honours deep and broad wherewith   20
Your Majesty loads our house. For those of old,
And the late dignities heap'd up to them,
We rest your hermits.[45]

Duncan
Where's the Thane of Cawdor?
We cours'd him at the heels and had a purpose   25
To be his purveyor;[46] but he rides well,
And his great love, sharp as his spur, hath holp[47] him
To his home before us. Fair and noble hostess,

[37] House martin or possibly a sparrow

[38] The bird's 'mansion' is his nest

[39] A part of a building which juts out

[40] A sculpted plaster decoration on the wall of a building

[41] A support or stone of brick

[42] Corner of a building

[43] The house martins have built their nests in all the castle's nooks and crannies. House martins were thought to be a good sign that a building was well-positioned and sheltered from the elements

[44] The bird lays its eggs in the nests it builds there

[45] Servants/subjects

[46] They tried to get there before Macbeth but failed

[47] Helped

MACBETH

41

We are your guest tonight.

Lady Macbeth Your servants ever 30
Have theirs, themselves, and what is theirs, in compt,[48]
To make their audit at your Highness' pleasure,
Still to return your own.

Duncan Give me your hand;
Conduct me to mine host. We love him highly, 35
And shall continue our graces towards him.
By your leave, hostess.

Exit

Art thou afeard
To be the same in thine own act and valour
As thou art in desire?

—LADY MACBETH (ACT I SCENE VII)

MACBETH

51

descendants) will be kings. ***Thou shalt get kings, though thou be none***. Obviously this is something Banquo would very much wish for. But while Banquo remains sceptical, knowing that the Witches cannot possibly bode good in the long run, Macbeth seems excited by their prophecy, and thus we are alerted to his 'vaulting ambition'. As Banquo observes: ***Good sir, why do you start, and seem to fear / Things that do sound so fair?*** By 'start' Banquo means that Macbeth has been physically shaken by the prophecy.

Next we learn that the Thane (Scottish Earl) of Cawdor is to be executed as a traitor. Duncan admits that he had no suspicions about Cawdor, and says that appearances can be deceptive: ***There's no art / To find the mind's construction in the face: / He was a gentleman on whom I built / An absolute trust.*** Macbeth receives Cawdor's title from Duncan as a reward for his bravery, but he seems to inherit the legacy of traitor with the thanedom as well. ***What he hath lost, noble Macbeth hath won.*** The first part of the Witches' prediction has come true, and this propels Macbeth into a kind of crazy ambition. He may have repressed his desire to be king thus far, but now his ambition seems tantalisingly close: ***Glamis, and Thane of Cawdor! / The greatest is behind.***

King Duncan greets Banquo and Macbeth warmly in Scene IV. It is immediately obvious to us that he is a good and decent king, grateful to these men, whom he trusts completely. Ironically, Duncan feels he hasn't fully appreciated Macbeth and says that he can never reward him enough: ***The sin of my ingratitude even now / Was heavy on me ... More is thy due than more than all can pay.***

Duncan's generous nature makes his murder all the more distressing.

In Scene V, Macbeth confides all his desires in a letter to his wife. The audience may question why he writes to his wife when he appears in person so soon afterwards, but this is for two good reasons. First, it tells us how close they are as marriage partners, when not all marriages at this time would have had such an equal balance of power. Second, the letter is used for dramatic effect. Lady Macbeth's reading of the letter is a strong visual spectacle: remember, the audience of the time would have been shocked to see a lady behave in this manner. Her cynical and manipulative response encourages us to see her as a heartless monster. She fears Macbeth is too nice to do what needs to be done: ***Yet I do fear thy nature. / It is too full o' the milk of human kindness / To catch the nearest way.***

She is plainly ambitious for her husband and gives us a valuable insight into his personality by telling us that she fears her husband's character will impede his ambition: ***Thou wouldst be great, / Art not without ambition, but without / The illness should attend it***. The 'illness' she refers to is the evil which needs to be in Macbeth's character in order for him to kill Duncan. Significantly, Lady Macbeth does not think her husband evil.

Duncan honours their household with an overnight stay, but Lady Macbeth resolves that he must be killed that very night to facilitate Macbeth's ascension to the throne of Scotland. ***The raven himself is hoarse / That croaks the fatal entrance of Duncan / Under my battlements***. She resolves to force Macbeth into overcoming his scruples about murdering Duncan. She advises him to **look like the innocent flower, / But be the serpent under it.** Lady Macbeth is well capable of deceit, and indeed she seems so much the loyal subject and gracious hostess that Duncan himself is charmed by her.

In Scene VII, when he is alone, Macbeth considers the implications of what he is about to do. Displaying the rashness which becomes his most consistent characteristic after the murder, he feels he should act quickly: **If it were done when 'tis done, then 'twere well / It were done quickly.**

The potential consequences are many. He may be found out and executed. He also knows that punishment will come in the afterlife. He knows, too, that Duncan is a good king who has only ever treated Macbeth with courtesy and consideration. However, he is consumed with an obsessive ambition and feels it is pointless to fight it: **I have no spur / To prick the sides of my intent, but only / Vaulting ambition, which o'erleaps itself / And falls on the other.** Macbeth knows that murder is a step too far. Like an overly eager rider vaulting on to a horse and missing the saddle, Macbeth is also aware that with this one evil deed he could lose the lofty position he already enjoys. This is a moment of insight, but Macbeth has altogether too few of these moments throughout the play.

Yet, just after this soliloquy, he abruptly tells his wife:
We will proceed no further in this business:
He hath honour'd me of late, and I have bought
Golden opinions from all sorts of people,
Which would be worn now in their newest gloss,
Not cast aside so soon.

The use of clothing imagery (which is repeated throughout the play) is very effective. Macbeth really does seem to think that all that it takes to be king is to wear a golden crown.

Sensing his hesitation, Lady Macbeth uses the full force of her persuasion to steel his resolve. She manipulates him easily because she knows him so well. She tells him to stop mulling over the murder and simply get on with it. She uses a horrific image to convince him that she would keep a promise she made to him, no matter what:

I have given suck and know
How tender 'tis to love the babe that milks me;
I would, while it was smiling in my face,
Have pluck'd my nipple from his boneless gums
And dash'd the brains out had I so sworn as you
Have done to this.

Later on in the play, of course, all Macbeth does is act without thinking of the consequences. Lady Macbeth, for her part, takes an active role in the murder by proposing to drug the Grooms and by laying out the daggers in readiness for the deed. There is no doubt that she, too, is culpable, but Macbeth has free will, and we cannot blame his wife for his crimes. The question of who is the more guilty will continue to occupy us in Act II.

Yet, at the end of Act I, it is Lady Macbeth who hatches the murder plot, and it is she, and the Witches, who give Macbeth the fateful push beyond the edge of morality into the heart of darkness.

MACBETH

53

IMPORTANT THEMES IN ACT I

• Ambition is defined as a strong desire to achieve or do something. Ambition is considered a positive trait nowadays, though not if it is pursued at the expense of one's moral code. In Shakespeare's day it was not in the interests of the rich if the poor were ambitious – and the vast majority of people were very poor. Instead, if you were a baker's son, it was expected that you would be a baker, too. Ambition threatened the status quo and could be severely punished. Macbeth's ambition is covetous and evil. He is intent on taking something that is not his to take. What is more, in this act he never actually explains why he even wants to be king.

• The theme of kingship is also established through the character of Duncan, who epitomises the qualities desirable in a king. He is kind, tolerant, trusting, but also firm, strategic and decisive. His only flaw is the trust he places in the wrong people. But perhaps Duncan's inability to see evil is due to the complete absence of that vice in him.

• The theme of evil is also explored throughout this act. Macbeth is trying to battle internally with his own predisposition to evil, though it seems clear that he will ultimately give in to it. Lady Macbeth's manipulation of her husband is evil, too. Evil is also explored externally, with the Witches as its physical manifestation. The dagger soliloquy in the next scene explores this theme further, and vividly shows that the difference between good and evil can often come down to one wrong decision or action.

CHARACTER DEVELOPMENT IN ACT I

• Macbeth seems heroic and patriotic, but ambition is his fatal flaw. The Witches' prophecy is the catalyst for his gradual descent into evil. He changes with each scene, his good characteristics fading as his negative traits come to the fore.

• Lady Macbeth is a repulsive character in this act. She is manipulative, duplicitous and sinister. As a woman, her character is particularly abhorrent. In this act, at least, she has no redeeming characteristics whatsoever.

• Banquo appears wholesome, sensible and devoted to his king. His character, in this act, stands as a rebuke to Macbeth, because his pragmatic reaction to the Witches is the one that Macbeth might have had, were it not for his fatal flaw.

QUESTIONS ON ACT 1

1. What is your first impression of the Witches?

2. Do you think a modern audience would react differently to the Witches than Shakespeare's audience did?

3. What do we learn about Macbeth in Scene II? What was your initial impression of him?

4. Write a diary entry from the perspective of one of the Scottish soldiers who witnessed Macbeth in action on the battlefield.

5. How does Macbeth echo the Witches in Scene II?

6. What are the main differences between how Macbeth reacts to the Witches and how Banquo reacts?

7. Why does Macbeth write to his wife, when he arrives just moments after she has read the letter?

8. Do you think Duncan is a good judge of character?

9. What was your first impression of Lady Macbeth?

10. What kind of marriage do you think Macbeth and Lady Macbeth have? Do you think it would have been typical of the time?

11. Pick out what you think are the ten best quotations from Act I and explain why you have chosen them. Make sure they cover a range of characters and themes.

12. Write a modern-day version of the letter which Macbeth sends Lady Macbeth.

MACBETH **ACT** 2

The ringing bell is Lady Macbeth's signal that all is ready. The bell ringing out in a silent theatre is meant to startle us. The audience is tense and nervous, wondering if Macbeth can possibly go through with such a terrible crime. Not only is this murder regicide, the killing of a king, it is also the killing of God's representative on earth, of Macbeth's guest, his commander in battle and his kinsman. It is a murder that is so wrong that it is no wonder it changes Macbeth fundamentally. The rhyming couplet at the end of the scene, in this instance, reminds us of the Witches: *I go, and it is done; the bell invites me. / Hear it not, Duncan, for it is a knell / That summons thee to heaven, or to hell.*

Is this a dagger which I see before me, The handle toward my hand? Come, let me clutch thee

– MACBETH

KEY **POINTS**

- *Banquo is bothered by the Witches' prophecy and is scared to sleep. Sleep symbolises innocence.*

- *The theme of kingship is again maintained through Duncan's gift.*

- *Macbeth decides to proceed with the murder, despite the consequences.*

- *Lady Macbeth rings the bell, a signal for the murder to take place.*

INVERNESS. COURTYARD OF MACBETH'S CASTLE

Enter Lady Macbeth

Lady Macbeth   That which hath made them drunk hath made me bold;
What hath quench'd them hath given me fire. Hark!
    Peace!
It was the owl that shriek'd, the fatal bellman,
Which gives the stern'st good night. He is about it.
The doors are open, and the surfeited[14] grooms   5
Do mock their charge with snores. I have drugg'd their
    possets[15]
That death and nature do contend about them,
Whether they live or die.

Macbeth   *[Within]* Who's there? What, ho!

Lady Macbeth   Alack,[16] I am afraid they have awak'd   10
And 'tis not done. The attempt and not the deed
Confounds us. Hark! I laid their daggers ready;
He could not miss 'em. Had he not resembled
My father as he slept, I had done 't.

Enter Macbeth

My husband!   15

Macbeth   I have done the deed. Didst thou not hear a noise?

Lady Macbeth   I heard the owl scream and the crickets cry.
Did not you speak?

Macbeth   When?

Lady Macbeth   Now.   20

Macbeth   As I descended?

Lady Macbeth   Ay.

Lady Macbeth needed some of the alcohol to give her the courage to carry out their plan. This shows she is not the black-hearted villain we originally thought

[14] *Drugged up*

[15] *Warm milk, with added alcohol to aid sleep*

[16] *Alas, or 'oh, no!'*

Macbeth	Hark! Who lies i' the second chamber?
Lady Macbeth	Donalbain. 25
Macbeth	This is a sorry sight. *[Looks on his hands]*
Lady Macbeth	A foolish thought, to say a sorry sight.
Macbeth	There's one did laugh in 's sleep, and one cried, 'Murder!' That they did wake each other. I stood and heard them, But they did say their prayers and address'd them 30 Again to sleep.
Lady Macbeth	There are two lodg'd together.
Macbeth	One cried, 'God bless us!' and 'Amen' the other, As they had seen me with these hangman's hands. Listening their fear, I could not say 'Amen,' 35 When they did say, 'God bless us!'
Lady Macbeth	Consider it not so deeply.
Macbeth	But wherefore could not I pronounce 'Amen'? I had most need of blessing, and 'Amen' Stuck in my throat. 40
Lady Macbeth	These deeds must not be thought After these ways; so, it will make us mad.
Macbeth	I heard a voice cry, 'Sleep no more! Macbeth does murder sleep' – the innocent sleep, Sleep that knits up the ravell'd sleave[17] of care, 45 The death of each day's life, sore labour's bath, Balm of hurt minds, great nature's second course, Chief nourisher in life's feast.
Lady Macbeth	What do you mean?

Sleep and prayer are associated with innocence. Now he is a murderer, Macbeth will not sleep, or pray, again. These lines mark the beginning of his realisation of the price we pay for doing wrong

[17] *Unravelled sleeve*

MACBETH

63

Macbeth   Still it cried, 'Sleep no more!' to all the house; 50
'Glamis hath murder'd sleep, and therefore Cawdor
Shall sleep no more. Macbeth shall sleep no more.'

Lady Macbeth   Who was it that thus cried? Why, worthy Thane,
You do unbend your noble strength, to think
So brainsickly of things. Go, get some water 55
And wash this filthy witness from your hand.
Why did you bring these daggers from the place?
They must lie there. Go carry them, and smear
The sleepy grooms with blood.

Macbeth   I'll go no more. 60
I am afraid to think what I have done;
Look on't again I dare not.

Lady Macbeth   Infirm of purpose!
Give me the daggers. The sleeping and the dead
Are but as pictures; 'tis the eye of childhood 65
That fears a painted devil. If he do bleed,
I'll gild[18] the faces of the grooms withal,
For it must seem their guilt.

Exit. Knocking within

Macbeth   Whence is that knocking?
How is't with me, when every noise appalls me? 70
What hands are here? Ha, they pluck out mine eyes!
Will all great Neptune's[19] ocean wash this blood
Clean from my hand? No, this my hand will rather
The multitudinous seas incarnadine,
Making the green one red. 75

Re-enter Lady Macbeth

Lady Macbeth   My hands are of your colour, but I shame
To wear a heart so white. *[Knocking within]* I hear
knocking
At the south entry. Retire we to our chamber.

[18] Cover their faces with blood. 'Gild' is fine gold leaf – Lady Macbeth is letting slip how precious Duncan's blood is, because he is a true king in every possible way

[19] Roman god of sea and water

A little water clears us of this deed.
How easy is it then! Your constancy   80
Hath left you unattended. *[Knocking within]* Hark, more
    knocking.
Get on your nightgown, lest occasion call us
And show us to be watchers. Be not lost
So poorly in your thoughts.

Macbeth   To know my deed, 'twere best not know myself.   85
[Knocking within]
Wake Duncan with thy knocking! I would thou couldst!

Exit

MODERN ENGLISH VERSION

INVERNESS, COURT OF MACBETH'S CASTLE

Enter Lady Macbeth

Lady Macbeth   I drugged the Grooms' bedtime milk. I had to drink some, too, to give myself some Dutch courage.

Macbeth   What the hell!

Lady Macbeth   Oh, no, what's going on? Did the Grooms wake? Were we not quick enough? I mean, I'd have done it myself, but Duncan so resembles my dad, I … I just couldn't.

Enter Macbeth

My husband!

Macbeth   I did it. Did you hear something, though?

Lady Macbeth   Just an owl hooting and crickets chirping.

Macbeth	When?
Lady Macbeth	Now.
Macbeth	As I came down?
Lady Macbeth	Yes.
Macbeth	Hold on, who is sleeping in the other bedroom?
Lady Macbeth	Donalbain.
Macbeth	Oh, God, look at my hands, they're covered in blood!
Lady Macbeth	So what?
Macbeth	One of the Grooms laughed in his sleep, and one cried 'Murder', but then they went back to sleep. One of them said, 'God bless us!' but I found I just could not say 'Amen'.
Lady Macbeth	Who cares?
Macbeth	But why couldn't I say 'Amen'? I needed a blessing, but 'Amen' just stuck in my throat!
Lady Macbeth	We need to forget about what we've done or we'll end up going mad.
Macbeth	I heard a voice cry, 'Sleep no more! Macbeth does murder sleep!' Am I never going to sleep again? Sleep is what soothes us, comforts us and heals us. Have I lost that forever?
Lady Macbeth	What do you mean?
Macbeth	No one in this castle will sleep again. 'Glamis has murdered sleep, so Cawdor has, too!'
Lady Macbeth	No one said that! Stop being so stupid and hysterical. Hey, wait! Why the hell did you bring the daggers with you? We

need to place them in the Grooms' hands so they will get the blame for the killing.

Macbeth
I don't care. I'm never going into that room again. I could not bear to look at the awful thing I have done. It would kill me.

Lady Macbeth
Don't be such a coward. The dead cannot hurt us. You're being childish. I'll bring the daggers back myself and smear the Grooms with blood, so they look as guilty as possible.

Macbeth
Oh, God! Who on earth is knocking on the gates? Jesus, I'm losing it; every little sound is terrifying me! Will my hands ever be clean again? There is so much blood on them that I think they are going to make the green sea red!

Re-enter Lady Macbeth

Lady Macbeth
My hands are red like yours, but I'd be embarrassed if I was as much of a coward as you are. All we need to do is wash our hands, and all this is forgotten. Come on, let's get into our nightclothes quickly and get to bed.

Macbeth
I don't think I can live with myself if I think too much about what I've done. I wish that knocking would wake Duncan! I wish it could!

Exit

INVERNESS. COURTYARD OF MACBETH'S CASTLE

Enter a Porter. Knocking within

Porter Here's a knocking indeed! If a man were porter
of Hell Gate, he should have old turning the key.[20]
[Knocking] Knock, knock, knock! Who's there,
i' the name of Beelzebub?[21] Here's a farmer that
hang'd himself on th' expectation of plenty. Come in   5
time! Have napkins enough about you; here you'll
sweat for't. *[Knocking]* Knock, knock! Who's
there, in th' other devil's name? Faith, here's an
equivocator[22] that could swear in both the scales
against either scale, who committed treason   10
enough for God's sake, yet could not equivocate to
heaven. O, come in, equivocator. *[Knocking]* Knock,
knock, knock! Who's there? Faith, here's an English tailor
come hither, for stealing out of a French hose.[23] Come in,
tailor; here you may roast your goose. *[Knocking]* Knock,   15
knock! Never at quiet! What are you? But this place is too
cold for hell. I'll devil-porter it no further. I had thought
to have let in some of all professions, that go the
primrose way to the everlasting bonfire. *[Knocking]*
Anon, anon! I pray you, remember the porter.   20

Opens the gate

Enter Macduff and Lennox

Macduff Was it so late, friend, ere you went to bed,
That you do lie so late?

Porter Faith, sir, we were carousing[24] till the second cock;[25]
and drink, sir, is a great provoker of three things.

Macduff What three things does drink especially provoke?   25

Porter Marry,[26] sir, nose-painting, sleep, and urine. Lechery,[27]
sir, it provokes, and unprovokes: it provokes the desire,
but it takes away the performance. Therefore, much drink

[20] *If a man were a porter of the gate to hell,
he'd grow old turning the key – meaning lots
of people go to hell, in the Porter's opinion*

[21] *Beelzebub is a slang name for the devil*

[22] *Liar*

[23] *Stockings (in Shakespeare's day, men wore
white woollen stockings under puffy shorts)*

*People who enjoy life, but sin
while they're doing so, were
said to be taking the 'primrose'
(nice) way to hell*

[24] *Partying* [25] *Until the early hours of the morning*

[26] *By Mary* [27] *Desire for sex*

may be said to be an equivocator[28] with lechery: it makes
him, and it mars him; it sets him on, and it takes him off; it   30
persuades him, and disheartens him; makes him stand to,
and not stand to; in conclusion, equivocates[29] him in a
sleep, and giving him the lie, leaves him.

Macduff   I believe drink gave thee the lie last night.

Porter   That it did, sir, i' the very throat on me; but I requited   35
him for his lie, and, I think, being too strong for him,
though he took up my legs sometime, yet I made shift
to cast him.

Macduff   Is thy master stirring?

Enter Macbeth

Our knocking has awaked him; here he comes.   40

Lennox   Good morrow, noble sir.

Macbeth   Good morrow, both.

Macduff   Is the King stirring, worthy Thane?

Macbeth   Not yet.

Macduff   He did command me to call timely on him;   45
I have almost slipp'd the hour.

Macbeth   I'll bring you to him.

Macduff   I know this is a joyful trouble to you,
But yet 'tis one.

Macbeth   The labour we delight in physics pain.[30]   50
This is the door.

Macduff   I'll make so bold to call,
For 'tis my limited service.

[28] Equaliser   *The Porter is saying that alcohol may make you lecherous, but it also takes away your ability to perform. Shakespeare's audience would have found this ribald humour very appealing. Then, as now, 'dirty jokes' were always popular!*

[29] Puts

[30] *The work we enjoy is not a burden*

MACBETH

69

ACT 2 SCENE III

Exit Macduff

Lennox   Goes the King hence today?

Macbeth   He does; he did appoint so.   55

Lennox reports that the night was stormy and strange, unnatural things were happening. In Shakespeare's day, people believed that when the weather was bad, it meant that some evil event was taking place. Significantly, the Witches always meet in bad weather, too

[31] Cries of pain

[32] Made noise all night

Lennox   The night has been unruly. Where we lay,
Our chimneys were blown down; and, as they say,
Lamentings[31] heard i' the air, strange screams of death,
And prophesying with accents terrible
Of dire combustion and confus'd events   60
New hatch'd to the woeful time. The obscure bird
Clamour'd the livelong night.[32] Some say the earth
Was feverous and did shake.

Macbeth   'Twas a rough night.

[33] Lennox says that he is young, but he cannot remember a worse night

Lennox   My young remembrance cannot parallel   65
A fellow to it.[33]

Re-enter Macduff

Macduff   O horror, horror, horror! Tongue nor heart
Cannot conceive nor name thee.

Macbeth/Lennox   What's the matter?

[34] Against God   [35] Open

Macduff   Confusion now hath made his masterpiece!   70
Most sacrilegious[34] murder hath broke ope[35]
The Lord's anointed temple and stole thence
The life o' the building.

Macbeth   What is't you say? The life?

Lennox   Mean you his Majesty?   75

[36] A monster, like Medusa, who turns those who look at her to stone. Meaning that anyone who sees Duncan's murdered body will be changed forever

Macduff   Approach the chamber, and destroy your sight
With a new Gorgon.[36] Do not bid me speak;
See, and then speak yourselves.

Exit Macbeth and Lennox

Awake, awake!
Ring the alarum bell. Murder and treason!   80
Banquo and Donalbain! Malcolm, awake!
Shake off this downy sleep, death's counterfeit,[37]
And look on death itself! Up, up, and see
The great doom's image! Malcolm! Banquo!
As from your graves rise up, and walk like sprites[38]   85
To countenance[39] this horror! Ring the bell.

Bell rings. Enter Lady Macbeth

Lady Macbeth   What's the business,
That such a hideous trumpet calls to parley[40]
The sleepers of the house? Speak, speak!

Macduff   O gentle lady,   90
'Tis not for you to hear what I can speak:
The repetition in a woman's ear
Would murder as it fell.

Enter Banquo

O Banquo, Banquo!
Our royal master's murder'd.   95

Lady Macbeth   Woe, alas!
What, in our house?

Banquo   Too cruel anywhere.
Dear Duff, I prithee, contradict thyself,
And say it is not so.   100

Re-enter Macbeth and Lennox, with Ross

Macbeth   Had I but died an hour before this chance,
I had lived a blessed time, for from this instant
There's nothing serious in mortality.

[37] *Imitation*

[38] *Ghosts or spirits*
[39] *Believe (when you see it)*

[40] *The alarm is waking everyone up with a shock*

Another example of dramatic irony. Macduff thinks that a woman should be spared the details of the murder, as she is too delicate to bear it. Little does he know how complicit Lady Macbeth is, for both she and Macbeth are putting on quite a show of innocence

41 Dregs

All is but toys; renown and grace is dead;
The wine of life is drawn, and the mere lees[41]   105
Is left this vault to brag of.

Enter Malcolm and Donalbain

Donalbain   What is amiss?

Macbeth   You are, and do not know 't.
The spring, the head, the fountain of your blood
Is stopp'd, the very source of it is stopp'd.   110

Macduff   Your royal father's murder'd.

Malcolm   O, by whom?

Lennox   Those of his chamber, as it seem'd, had done 't.

42 Covered

Their hands and faces were all badg'd[42] with blood;
So were their daggers, which unwip'd we found   115
Upon their pillows.
They star'd, and were distracted; no man's life
Was to be trusted with them.

Macbeth   O, yet I do repent me of my fury,
That I did kill them.   120

Macduff   Wherefore did you so?

43 Restrained

Macbeth   Who can be wise, amaz'd, temperate[43] and furious,
Loyal and neutral, in a moment? No man.
The expedition of my violent love
Outrun the pauser, reason. Here lay Duncan,   125
His silver skin lac'd with his golden blood,
And his gash'd stabs look'd like a breach in nature
For ruin's wasteful entrance; there, the murderers,
Steep'd in the colours of their trade, their daggers

44 Covered

Unmannerly breech'd[44] with gore. Who could refrain,   130
That had a heart to love, and in that heart
Courage to make 's love known?

Lady Macbeth	Help me hence, ho!	
Macduff	Look to the lady.	
Malcolm	*[Aside to Donalbain]* Why do we hold our tongues,	135
	That most may claim this argument for ours?[45]	
Donalbain	*[Aside to Malcolm]*	
	What should be spoken here where our fate,	
	Hid in an auger[46] hole, may rush and seize us?	
	Let's away,	
	Our tears are not yet brew'd.[47]	140
Malcolm	*[Aside to Donalbain]* Nor our strong sorrow	
	Upon the foot of motion.	
Banquo	Look to the lady.	
	Lady Macbeth is carried out	
	And when we have our naked frailties hid,	
	That suffer in exposure, let us meet	145
	And question this most bloody piece of work,	
	To know it further. Fears and scruples shake us.	
	In the great hand of God I stand, and thence	
	Against the undivulg'd[48] pretence I fight	
	Of treasonous malice.	150
Macduff	And so do I.	
All	So all.	
Macbeth	Let's briefly put on manly readiness	
	And meet i' the hall together.	
All	Well contented.	155
	Exit all but Malcolm and Donalbain	

Lady Macbeth's faint distracts attention from Macbeth's killing of the Grooms before they could be questioned

[45] *Malcolm asks why he and Donalbain are silent, when they are the ones who have most right to speak, as Duncan was their father*

[46] *Deep*

[47] *They are too shocked to cry*

[48] *What is not yet known*

MACBETH

73

Malcolm	What will you do? Let's not consort with them.
	To show an unfelt sorrow is an office
	Which the false man does easy. I'll to England.
Donalbain	To Ireland, I; our separated fortune
	Shall keep us both the safer. Where we are
	There's daggers in men's smiles; the near in blood,
	The nearer bloody.
Malcolm	This murderous shaft that's shot
	Hath not yet lighted, and our safest way
	Is to avoid the aim. Therefore to horse;
	And let us not be dainty of leave-taking,
	But shift away. There's warrant in that theft
	Which steals itself when there's no mercy left.

160

165

Malcolm says that they are justified in 'stealing' their freedom because there is no mercy left, i.e. they are in danger

Exit

THIS IS A VERY important scene. It begins, surprisingly, with humour, the last thing the audience is expecting. This is an example of Shakespeare's fantastic pacing. We are still reeling from Duncan's murder, and the original audience, who were governed by a monarch, would have been particularly shocked to witness regicide, even on stage. However, the Porter's ribald humour provides comic relief. The dramatic function of this interlude is to offer a contrast with what has just transpired. It also lulls the audience into a brief moment of happiness before the harrowing action that follows.

Here lay Duncan,
His silver skin lac'd with his golden blood,
And his gash'd stabs look'd like a breach in nature
— MACBETH

We are also introduced to Macduff. He is the Thane of Fife, and the similarity between his name and Macbeth's is quite deliberate. His role in the play is to act as a foil to Macbeth.

The Porter and Macduff exchange some light-hearted words when he arrives to collect Duncan: *I believe drink gave thee the lie last night.* It is a tense, suspenseful moment for the audience, as we wait for Macduff to make his discovery, but it is also funny. Shakespeare is toying expertly with our emotions.

When we last saw Macbeth, he was disoriented, remorseful and confused. Shakespeare may have intended us to think that he would look so guilty that he would immediately be found out. If so, we get a shock when Macbeth appears. He cheerfully greets Macduff and lies casually – *The labour we delight in physics pain* – about the pleasure he takes in serving Duncan.

The Witches do not appear in the scene, but Lennox remarks upon the tumultuous storm that raged that night: *The night has been unruly. Where we lay, / Our chimneys were blown down; and, as they say, / Lamentings heard i' the air, strange screams of death.* The bad weather reminds us that the Witches were close by, perhaps influencing events, or perhaps just enjoying observing an evil act which they had helped to set in motion.

Macduff's reaction to Duncan's death is sincere and heartfelt: *O horror, horror, horror! Tongue nor heart / Cannot conceive nor name thee.* Macbeth, by contrast, is a consummate liar. He puts on a great show of grief. In fact, he probably overdoes it, as people often do when they are lying. His words are melodramatic and self-conscious:

> *Here lay Duncan,*
> *His silver skin lac'd with his golden blood,*
> *And his gash'd stabs look'd like a breach in nature.*

Lady Macbeth is similarly convincing, and there is a moment of black humour when Macduff says: *O gentle lady, / 'Tis*

not for you to hear what I can speak: / The repetition in a woman's ear / Would murder as it fell. Like any gentleman of Shakespeare's day, Macduff thinks of women as gentle and innocent. This illustrates the theme of gender and the link between gender and violence.

One tactical mistake Macbeth makes is to kill the Grooms: *O, yet I do repent me of my fury, / That I did kill them.* The Grooms would have been killed eventually; a servant's life was not valued very highly in those times. But first they would have been questioned, and in Shakespeare's day the most awful forms of torture were used to extract the truth. Macbeth justifies himself, saying he killed them out of loyalty to Duncan, but, as we will later see, his actions are enough to awaken the suspicions of Macduff: *Wherefore did you so?*

At this precise moment, Lady Macbeth faints, conveniently distracting attention from her husband. She may be starting to show signs of remorse, or she may be manipulating the situation to her own advantage. We still do not know enough about her to be sure, either way.

Banquo seems as shocked as Macduff, and it is he who insists they investigate the murder fully: *let us meet / And question this most bloody piece of work, / To know it further.* At this point, it is impossible to know if Banquo suspects anything. We will have to wait until Act III for this to be revealed.

However, Duncan was not childless. He has left two sons, one of whom he had specifically appointed as his successor. Was Macbeth going to kill Malcolm and Donalbain, too? This is a point in the play where we may have to 'suspend our disbelief' (not question convenient events). It is, in any case, convenient that Malcolm and Donalbain realise that they will be the chief suspects, as they had most to gain from Duncan's death. They are certainly correct in guessing that their lives are also in danger: *Where we are / There's daggers in men's smiles; the near in blood, / The nearer bloody.* But by fleeing (Malcolm to England, Donalbain to Ireland), the final obstacles to Macbeth's royal ambitions are no more, and the way is clear for him to become king.

KEY **POINTS**

- *Committing murder irrevocably alters Macbeth's character. He kills two more innocent people in this scene, which proves how much he has changed.*

- *Malcolm shows himself to be his father's son when he is astute enough to realise the danger and flee. This also explores the theme of kingship.*

- *The cracks have started to appear in Lady Macbeth's character. She drinks for courage, can't kill Duncan herself and (perhaps) faints from shock.*

- *Macduff is suspicious of Macbeth.*

OUTSIDE MACBETH'S CASTLE

Enter Ross with an Old Man

Old Man	Threescore and ten[49] I can remember well,
	Within the volume of which time I have seen
	Hours dreadful and things strange, but this sore night
	Hath trifled former knowings.[50]
Ross	Ah, good father, 5
	Thou seest the heavens, as troubled with man's act,
	Threaten his bloody stage. By the clock 'tis day,
	And yet dark night strangles the travelling lamp.
	Is't night's predominance,[51] or the day's shame,
	That darkness does the face of earth entomb,[52] 10
	When living light should kiss it?
Old Man	'Tis unnatural,
	Even like the deed that's done. On Tuesday last
	A falcon, towering in her pride of place,
	Was by a mousing owl hawk'd at and kill'd.[53] 15
Ross	And Duncan's horses – a thing most strange and certain –
	Beauteous and swift, the minions[54] of their race,
	Turn'd wild in nature, broke their stalls, flung out,
	Contending 'gainst obedience, as they would make
	War with mankind. 20
Old Man	'Tis said they eat each other.[55]
Ross	They did so, to the amazement of mine eyes
	That look'd upon't.

Enter Macduff

	Here comes the good Macduff.
	How goes the world, sir, now? 25
Macduff	Why, see you not?

[49] A score is 20. If he is three-score and ten, then he is 70 years old

[50] This stormy night has been so bad it has made all other storms seem pathetic

Now, following Duncan's murder, it is dark when it should be light. The natural order of things has been reversed by Macbeth's usurpation. Perhaps this is also what the Witches meant when they said 'Fair is foul and foul is fair'

[51] Domination

[52] Enclose like a grave

[53] A falcon, a mighty bird of prey, was killed by a small owl. This is against the natural order of things. It is also symbolic. Duncan is the falcon and Macbeth the owl, lesser than Duncan in every possible way

[54] Best

[55] Duncan's horses ate each other – a symbol of the 'dog eat dog' mentality that Macbeth's reign will bring

	Ross	Is't known who did this more than bloody deed?
[56] *The Grooms*	**Macduff**	Those that Macbeth hath slain.[56]
	Ross	Alas, the day! What good could they pretend? 30
[57] *Bribed*	**Macduff**	They were suborn'd:[57] Malcolm and Donalbain, the King's two sons, Are stol'n away and fled, which puts upon them Suspicion of the deed.

Ross laments how ambition could make someone commit the crime of killing the person who gave you life. He is talking about Malcolm and Donalbain, but may be speaking sarcastically, if he is not convinced of their guilt

[58] *Plunder*

[59] *The crown*

	Ross	'Gainst nature still! 35 Thriftless ambition, that wilt ravin[58] up Thine own life's means! Then 'tis most like The sovereignty[59] will fall upon Macbeth.
[60] *Scone is where the ancient kings of Scotland were crowned*	**Macduff**	He is already named, and gone to Scone[60] To be invested. 40
	Ross	Where is Duncan's body?
[61] *Burial place for the kings of Scotland*	**Macduff**	Carried to Colmekill,[61] The sacred storehouse of his predecessors And guardian of their bones.
	Ross	Will you to Scone? 45
[62] *Macduff is the Thane of Fife, so he is going home*	**Macduff**	No, cousin, I'll to Fife.[62]
	Ross	Well, I will thither.
	Macduff	Well, may you see things well done there: adieu! Lest our old robes sit easier than our new!
	Ross	Farewell, father. 50
[63] *Blessing and protection*	**Old Man**	God's benison[63] go with you, and with those That would make good of bad and friends of foes!

Exit

WHILE SHORT, AND fundamentally serving only to advance the plot, this scene is also rich in imagery and atmosphere. Light and darkness are important motifs in *Macbeth*. We learn that there is no daylight now, only constant darkness, a turn of events that recalls both Macbeth's and Lady Macbeth's pleas for darkness. Night represents evil, while day represents goodness. Duncan's death was like the death of daylight itself. Nature is rebelling against Macbeth's unnatural usurpation.

Along with the lack of daylight, the weather has become erratic, and even animals are reacting to the fundamental wrongness of Duncan's murder. His beautiful horses attack and eat each other. An owl catches a falcon, when usually it is the falcon that preys on the owl.

We learn that Duncan's body is to be interred at Colmekill, the traditional resting place of the Scottish kings. Meantime, everyone has assumed that Malcolm's and Donalbain's hasty departures are proof of their guilt. Macbeth is to be crowned.

Macduff deliberately snubs Macbeth's coronation: **No, cousin, I'll to Fife.** This will alert Macbeth to Macduff's opinion of him. Macduff, incidentally, also uses clothing imagery to suggest that Macbeth's kingship might not be as successful as Duncan's: **Adieu, / Lest our old robes sit easier than our new!**

Is't night's predominance, or the day's shame,
That darkness does the face of earth entomb,
When living light should kiss it?

– ROSS

KEY **POINTS**

- *Note the variety of imagery in this scene: nature, clothing and storm.*

- *Nature is rebelling against Macbeth's unlawful reign.*

- *A 'dog eat dog' mentality is now the norm in Scotland.*

- *Macduff's dramatic function is twofold. He is a foil to Macbeth and a symbol of hope for the dark times ahead.*

FOCUS ON ACT 2

'Almost from the beginning of this act, Macbeth's character declines. In an incredibly tense soliloquy, he visualises a dagger, first clean, then bloody'

THIS DRAMATIC and disturbing act revolves around the murder of Duncan and its immediate aftermath. The way the characters develop subsequently is further evidence of Shakespeare's brilliance. There is a gradual and wholly believable change in Lady Macbeth and Banquo, but a more abrupt change in Macbeth, suggesting that he has become unhinged. Macbeth had to go against all his instincts in order to kill Duncan, and now it seems that for him there is no way back.

The insidious nature of evil is seen in Banquo's gradual decline into obsessing about the Witches. He is the last person Macbeth speaks to before the murder. Banquo gives him a diamond for Lady Macbeth, a present from the great Duncan. The purity of the diamond, its transparency and value, is symbolic of Duncan's exemplary character and kingship. Banquo tells Macbeth that he has dreamed of *the three weird sisters: / To you they have show'd some truth.* They agree to meet and discuss the Witches soon. Banquo obviously has some ambitions, too, but how far would he have gone to achieve them?

Almost from the beginning of this act, Macbeth's character declines. In an incredibly tense soliloquy, he visualises a dagger, first clean, then bloody. This dagger is the manifestation of a guilty conscience. Yet, though his conscience already plagues him, Macbeth cannot foresee how he will feel later on. He is in a state of disbelief at this point, but gathers himself when he hears the bell, the signal from his wife that she has readied the murder scene: *I go, and it is done; the bell invites me. / Hear it not, Duncan, for it is a knell / That summons thee to heaven, or to hell.*

Scene II is as tense and harrowing as a murder scene could be. Lady Macbeth seemed almost witch-like in Act I, but in this scene she displays some vulnerability. She takes some of the Grooms' drink to fortify herself – *That which hath made them drunk hath made me bold* – a move that is quite a surprise, considering how monstrous she has appeared thus far. She lays out the daggers for Macbeth, as arranged, and claims she would have done the deed herself except for the fact that Duncan looked like her father: *Had he not resembled / My father as he slept, I had done 't.* But this is not a valid excuse – old men look quite similar in some ways. What is more likely is that Lady Macbeth simply could not kill Duncan. Her later appearances in the play will support this theory. However much she may have encouraged her husband, ultimately Lady Macbeth could not stab Duncan to death. Macbeth could, and that is the fundamental difference between the two.

Lady Macbeth is anxious about her husband's return; hardly surprising as there is no way of telling how a person will react after such an event. For all her intuition, she cannot see that the Macbeth who went in to kill Duncan will never return. You cannot kill for the worst of all possible motives and not lose something of yourself, of your soul, in the process.

When Macbeth emerges from Duncan's chamber, he is distraught, utterly horrified at what he has done:

> *'Sleep no more!*
> *Macbeth does murder sleep' – the innocent sleep,*
> *Sleep that knits up the ravell'd sleave of care,*
> *The death of each day's life, sore labour's bath,*

That which hath made them drunk hath made me bold

– LADY MACBETH (ACT II SCENE II)

Balm of hurt minds, great nature's second course,
Chief nourisher in life's feast.

Sleep is a recurring motif in the play. An inability to sleep is associated with guilt. Macbeth is certain he will never have a peaceful night's sleep again, and that a lack of sleep can make a sane person crazy. He knows he will never have a moment's peace from this point on. It is interesting that he still doesn't think of Duncan, but is concerned with himself, what he has lost, and the price he will pay.

In Macbeth's agitated state he makes the mistake of bringing the bloody murder weapons with him. *Why did you bring these daggers from the place?* His wife orders him to return: *Go carry them, and smear / The sleepy grooms with blood.* For the first time, perhaps, he does not obey her. *I'll go no more. / I am afraid to think what I have done; / Look on't again I dare not.* Macbeth's crumbling resolve seems to strengthen Lady Macbeth's, and she appears to return to her previous, determined persona:

Give me the daggers. The sleeping and the dead
Are but as pictures; 'tis the eye of childhood
That fears a painted devil. If he do bleed,
I'll gild the faces of the grooms withal,
For it must seem their guilt.

Given that the murder of Duncan is so central to the action of the play, it may seem surprising that it takes place off stage. Perhaps Shakespeare knew that nothing the actors could physically demonstrate could equal the power of the audience's imagination to visualise Duncan's brutal murder. Many film versions do show the killing, because special effects make it easy to create a realistic death scene that is not so easily achieved in the theatre.

After Lady Macbeth places the daggers by the sleeping Grooms and smears their faces with blood, she challenges Macbeth's manliness to make him get a grip on his emotions: *My hands are of your colour, but I shame / To wear a heart so white.* This emasculating of her husband is obviously a technique which works. For although Macbeth is still full of remorse – *Wake Duncan with thy knocking! I would thou couldst!* – it is apparent in the next scene that his wife's words have enabled him to pull himself together.

After a comic interlude provided by the Porter's bawdy monologue (Shakespeare's audience loved ribald humour), Macduff arrives to call on Duncan. This is a crucial point in the play, for now we will see what Macbeth is really like. Will he break down and confess or will he follow through on his crimes? When Macduff finds Duncan's body, we learn what Macbeth, changed utterly by the terrible thing he has done, is capable of. He lies convincingly: *Confusion now hath made his masterpiece! / Most sacrilegious murder hath broke ope / The Lord's anointed temple and stole thence / The life o' the building.* With a chilling callousness, he also kills the innocent Grooms, making sure they do not have the chance to defend themselves against the charge of murder. Macduff, even in his grief over the death of Duncan, registers surprise at Macbeth's excessive force: *Wherefore did you so?*

Lady Macbeth faints at this point. Many critics presume that this is to distract attention from her husband. But is this necessarily the case? Perhaps she faints in genuine horror at what Macbeth is capable of. The fact that she later kills herself out of guilt supports this view. However, either theory is valid.

FORRES. THE PALACE

Enter Banquo

Banquo Thou hast it now: King, Cawdor, Glamis, all,
As the weird women[1] promis'd, and I fear
Thou play'dst most foully for't; yet it was said
It should not stand in thy posterity,
But that myself should be the root and father   5
Of many kings. If there come truth from them
– As upon thee, Macbeth, their speeches shine –
Why, by the verities on thee made good,
May they not be my oracles as well,
And set me up in hope? But hush, no more.   10

[1] *Witches*

*Sennet[2] sounds. Enter Macbeth as King, Lady Macbeth
as Queen, Lennox, Ross, Lords, Ladies, and Attendants*

[2] *Trumpet*

Macbeth Here's our chief guest.

Lady Macbeth If he had been forgotten,
It had been as a gap in our great feast,
And all thing unbecoming.

Macbeth Tonight we hold a solemn supper, sir,   15
And I'll request your presence.

Banquo Let your Highness
Command upon me, to the which my duties
Are with a most indissoluble[3] tie
For ever knit.   20

[3] *Unbreakable*

Macbeth Ride you this afternoon?

Banquo Ay, my good lord.

Macbeth We should have else desir'd your good advice,
Which still hath been both grave and prosperous
In this day's council; but we'll take tomorrow.   25

Is't far you ride?

Banquo As far, my lord, as will fill up the time
'Twixt this and supper. Go not my horse the better,
I must become a borrower of the night
For a dark hour or twain.[4]   30

Macbeth Fail not our feast.

Banquo My lord, I will not.

Macbeth We hear our bloody cousins are bestow'd
In England and in Ireland, not confessing
Their cruel parricide,[5] filling their hearers
With strange invention. But of that tomorrow,   35
When therewithal we shall have cause of state
Craving us jointly. Hie you to horse; adieu,
Till you return at night. Goes Fleance with you?

Banquo Ay, my good lord. Our time does call upon 's.

Macbeth I wish your horses swift and sure of foot,   40
And so I do commend you to their backs.
Farewell.

Exit Banquo

Let every man be master of his time
Till seven at night; to make society
The sweeter welcome, we will keep ourself   45
Till supper time alone. While then, God be with you!

Exit all but Macbeth and an Attendant

Sirrah, a word with you. Attend those men
Our pleasure?

Attendant They are, my lord, without the palace gate.

It will later prove very significant that Banquo promises to attend the feast

[4] Banquo's journey is long, so he will have to ride for an hour or two in darkness. Most people didn't travel at night, as it was far too dangerous. They would not just have been fearful of highwaymen, etc., but also of witches and ghosts

[5] The murder of a parent

BANQUO'S FIRST WORDS show that he knows what Macbeth has done, and while he certainly seems disapproving, he stays silent, and does not alert the royal court to his suspicions: *Thou hast it now: King, Cawdor, Glamis, all, / As the weird women promis'd, and I fear / Thou play'dst most foully for't*. Banquo's silence is treasonous, as well as a serious moral lapse on his part. More disturbing still, Banquo does not think of poor Duncan, but of whether the prophecy relating to him will come true: *May they not be my oracles as well, / And set me up in hope?*

Neither does Banquo challenge Macbeth with his suspicions, but instead promises him loyalty. *Let your Highness / Command upon me, to the which my duties / Are with a most indissoluble tie / For ever knit.* Perhaps Banquo's loyalty is to a friend at this point, but loyalty to your king should supersede all others. When Macbeth talks about

Thou hast it now: King, Cawdor, Glamis, all,
As the weird women promis'd

– BANQUO

Duncan's 'killers', he draws Banquo into further complicity: *We hear our bloody cousins are bestow'd / In England and in Ireland, not confessing / Their cruel parricide.*

Macbeth seems to take an unusual interest in Banquo's travelling plans for the day, and Banquo readily informs him of where exactly he will be, blithely telling a man he knows to be a killer that he may have to ride for an hour or two in darkness. Macbeth responds by rather threateningly telling

Banquo to make sure he is at the royal banquet that night: **Fail not our feast.**

The conversation between Banquo and Macbeth seems friendly enough. But, as soon as Banquo exits, Macbeth reveals his real thoughts: **To be thus is nothing, / But to be safely thus. Our fears in Banquo / Stick deep.** Macbeth has the crown he so ardently desired, but he is still not content. He is paranoid about Banquo and bitterly resentful of the fact that it is his offspring who will inherit the throne for which he has paid so dearly. **They hail'd him father to a line of kings. / Upon my head they plac'd a fruitless crown / And put a barren sceptre in my gripe.** Macbeth's lack of children distresses him. But while his disappointment at being childless is understandable, his violent reaction to the situation is not.

When an attendant announces that visitors have arrived, we presume they are guests for the banquet. The last thing we expect is that Macbeth has hired assassins to have his best friend and comrade in battle, and his young son, Fleance, killed.

This is Macbeth's very first act as king. Significantly, he does not include Lady Macbeth in his plans. Their awful crime has not brought them closer together but is the catalyst for their growing apart. Subsequently, Macbeth does not agonise over Banquo's death in the way he did over Duncan's, and yet Banquo's is far more personal, as he is Macbeth's closest friend. Macbeth is becoming a monster, and, in the rhyming couplet which closes the scene, we can see that his speech is becoming more and more reminiscent of the Witches': **It is concluded: Banquo, thy soul's flight, / If it find heaven, must find it out tonight.**

KEY **POINTS**

- *Banquo does not speak out about his suspicions. His crime is one of omission.*

- *Macbeth's moral disintegration continues at an alarming rate.*

- *The killing of Banquo is Macbeth's first act as king. This shows the potential of kingship to be a force for evil if the king himself is evil.*

THE PALACE

Enter Lady Macbeth and a Servant

Lady Macbeth　Is Banquo gone from court?

Servant　Ay, madam, but returns again tonight.

Lady Macbeth　Say to the King I would attend his leisure
For a few words.

Servant　Madam, I will.　　　　　　　　　5

Exit

Lady Macbeth　Nought's had, all's spent,
Where our desire is got without content.
'Tis safer to be that which we destroy
Than by destruction dwell in doubtful joy.

Enter Macbeth

How now, my lord? Why do you keep alone,　　10
Of sorriest fancies your companions making,
Using those thoughts which should indeed have died
With them they think on? Things without all remedy
Should be without regard. What's done is done.

Macbeth　We have scotch'd[17] the snake, not kill'd it.　　15
She'll close and be herself, whilst our poor malice
Remains in danger of her former tooth.
But let the frame of things disjoint, both the worlds suffer,
Ere we will eat our meal in fear and sleep
In the affliction of these terrible dreams　　20
That shake us nightly. Better be with the dead,
Whom we, to gain our peace, have sent to peace,
Than on the torture of the mind to lie
In restless ecstasy. Duncan is in his grave;
After life's fitful fever he sleeps well.[18]　　25

Lady Macbeth is beginning to wonder what they did it all for, if Macbeth still is not happy

[17] Slashed

[18] Macbeth is still jealous of Duncan, now because he is sleeping peacefully!

MACBETH

95

ACT 3 SCENE II

Macbeth echoes his wife's words. But he says it is better to continue to kill or you may as well be dead, whereas Lady Macbeth wants to move on from murder and enjoy their lives again

Treason has done his worst; nor steel, nor poison,
Malice domestic, foreign levy, nothing,
Can touch him further.

Lady Macbeth Come on,
Gentle my lord, sleek o'er your rugged looks; 30
Be bright and jovial among your guests tonight.

Macbeth So shall I, love, and so, I pray, be you.
Let your remembrance apply to Banquo;
Present him eminence, both with eye and tongue:
Unsafe the while, that we 35
Must lave our honours in these flattering streams,
And make our faces vizards[19] to our hearts,
Disguising what they are.

Lady Macbeth You must leave this.

Macbeth O, full of scorpions is my mind, dear wife! 40
Thou know'st that Banquo and his Fleance lives.

Lady Macbeth But in them nature's copy's not eterne.[20]

Macbeth There's comfort yet; they are assailable.
Then be thou jocund. Ere the bat hath flown
His cloister'd flight, ere to black Hecate's summons 45
The shard-borne beetle with his drowsy hums
Hath rung night's yawning peal, there shall be done
A deed of dreadful note.

Lady Macbeth What's to be done?

Macbeth Be innocent of the knowledge, dearest chuck,[21] 50
Till thou applaud the deed. Come, seeling night,
Scarf up the tender eye of pitiful day,[22]
And with thy bloody and invisible hand
Cancel and tear to pieces that great bond
Which keeps me pale! Light thickens, and the crow 55
Makes wing to the rooky wood;

[19] *Visors or masks – meaning their faces will not reveal what is in their hearts (note appearance versus reality)*

[20] *Banquo and Fleance won't live forever*

[21] *Chicken – a term of endearment, like 'pet' or 'sweetheart'*

[22] *'Seeling' is stitching a falcon's eyelids to make them tame. So Macbeth is using this violent image to ask the night to stitch up day's eyes, i.e. to make it dark*

MACBETH

96

Good things of day begin to droop and drowse,
Whiles night's black agents to their preys do rouse.
Thou marvell'st at my words, but hold thee still:
Things bad begun make strong themselves by ill. 60
So, prithee, go with me.

Exit

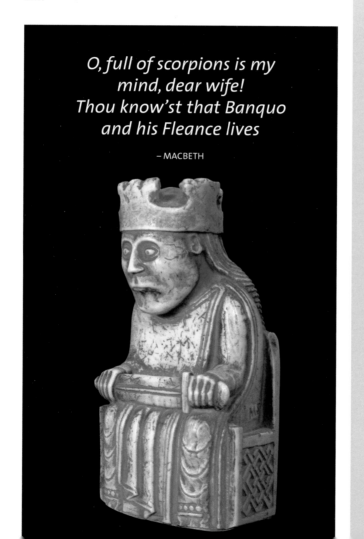

*O, full of scorpions is my
mind, dear wife!
Thou know'st that Banquo
and his Fleance lives*

– MACBETH

SCENE **ANALYSIS**

IN THIS SCENE, we note that Macbeth's language continues to change dramatically. He constantly alludes to darkness, death and evil. His words are disturbing and ominous.

> *Ere the bat hath flown*
> *His cloister'd flight, ere to black Hecate's summons*
> *The shard-borne beetle with his drowsy hums*
> *Hath rung night's yawning peal, there shall be done*
> *A deed of dreadful note.*

Macbeth seems to be actively embracing the dark side, not just of his own personality but of humanity itself. He is also distancing his wife from him by not telling her of his plans.

Lady Macbeth also seems different. Her language is gentler, softer: ***Things without all remedy / Should be without regard. What's done is done.*** She wants to move on. It really seems as if she thought they could kill Duncan and then return to normal life. For her part, Lady Macbeth does not seem to care about being queen; she never mentions it. So perhaps she involved herself in the murder purely for Macbeth's benefit. In this scene, it is obvious how much she loves her husband: ***Gentle my lord, sleek o'er your rugged looks; / Be bright and jovial among your guests tonight.*** She continues to do her best to help him in his new role.

It is almost as if the couple are reversing roles. Earlier, Lady Macbeth seemed shockingly evil, though she had some signs of goodness, however small. Macbeth – the conquering hero, brave warrior and devoted husband – always had the fatal flaw of ambition, but he did try to suppress it. He changed his mind about killing Duncan, and it is reasonable to argue that he would have drawn back from the brink had his wife not manipulated him. But she did manipulate him, and he did murder Duncan, and now he cannot return to being the man he once was.

Macbeth becomes paranoid and even less able to master his willingness to commit evil. The fact that he needs to justify Banquo's death shows that he is not yet wholly evil, but at the same time is very far from redemption. He does not reveal his plans to his wife, saying only: ***Be innocent of the knowledge, dearest chuck, / Till thou applaud the deed.***

KEY **POINTS**

- *Macbeth and Lady Macbeth are growing apart. She wants to resume normal life, and he wants to continue to kill.*

- *The confidantes of Acts I and II are no more. Macbeth now excludes his wife from his plans. Her words do not seem to have any effect on him now, whereas previously he was very much persuaded by her.*

A PARK NEAR THE PALACE

Enter three Murderers

First Murderer	But who did bid thee join with us?
Third Murderer	Macbeth.
Second Murderer	He needs not our mistrust, since he delivers Our offices and what we have to do To the direction just.

First Murderer	Then stand with us. The west yet glimmers with some streaks of day; Now spurs the lated[23] traveller apace To gain the timely inn, and near approaches The subject of our watch.	

Third Murderer	Hark! I hear horses.
Banquo	*[Within]* Give us a light there, ho!
Second Murderer	Then 'tis he; the rest That are within the note of expectation Already are i' the court.
First Murderer	His horses go about.
Third Murderer	Almost a mile, but he does usually, So all men do, from hence to the palace gate Make it their walk.
Second Murderer	A light, a light!

Enter Banquo and Fleance with a torch

Third Murderer	'Tis he.
First Murderer	Stand to't.

[23] *Delayed*

5

10

15

20

MACBETH

99

ACT 3 SCENE III

Banquo	It will be rain tonight.
First Murderer	Let it come down.
	They set upon Banquo
Banquo	O, treachery! Fly, good Fleance, fly, fly, fly! 25 Thou mayst revenge. O slave!
	Dies. Fleance escapes
Third Murderer	Who did strike out the light?
First Murderer	Was 't not the way?
Third Murderer	There's but one down; the son is fled.
Second Murderer	We have lost 30 Best half of our affair.
First Murderer	Well, let's away, and say how much is done.
	Exit

LIKE MANY OTHER scenes, this one is primarily visual. It might not seem very dramatic on the page, but when it is acted out it is really exciting. The Murderers lie in wait for Banquo. Strangely, a third Murderer appears. The identity of this third man is unclear. There are three theories.

1. *The paranoid Macbeth sent another hired assassin to make sure the job was done right.*

2. *It is a textual error made by a scribe or printer. Shakespeare's work was scarcely published during his own lifetime and was often altered in later years. It could also have been Shakespeare's own mistake, as many of his plays were improvised, with lines added or scored out depending on the reaction of the audience. It might even have been to give a part to an actor whose role had been killed off.*

3. *It is Macbeth himself (this is unlikely).*

The murder is frenzied and confusing. Banquo's concern is for his son, who does indeed manage to escape. ***O, treachery! Fly, good Fleance, fly, fly, fly! / Thou mayst revenge.*** The botched murder attempt creates a sense of dread. We can only imagine Macbeth's response to Fleance's escape.

KEY **POINT**

* *Banquo is killed but Fleance escapes, suggesting that the prophecy (which so bothers Macbeth) may still come true.*

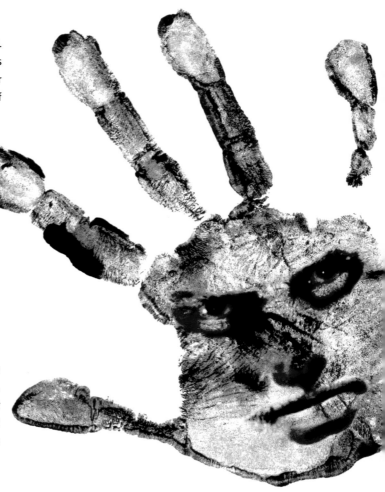

A HALL IN THE PALACE. A BANQUET PREPARED

*Enter Macbeth, Lady Macbeth, Ross, Lennox, Lords,
and Attendants*

²⁴ *Their social level. The higher in
rank you were, the closer you
could sit to the king*

Macbeth   You know your own degrees;²⁴ sit down.
At first and last the hearty welcome.

Lords   Thanks to your Majesty.

Macbeth   Ourself will mingle with society
And play the humble host.   5
Our hostess keeps her state, but in best time
We will require her welcome.

Lady Macbeth   Pronounce it for me, sir, to all our friends,
For my heart speaks they are welcome.

Enter First Murderer to the door

Macbeth   See, they encounter thee with their hearts' thanks.   10
Both sides are even; here I'll sit i' the midst.
²⁵ *Laughter*
Be large in mirth;²⁵ anon we'll drink a measure
The table round. *[Approaches the door]* There's blood
          upon thy face.

Murderer   'Tis Banquo's then.

Macbeth   'Tis better thee without than he within.   15
Is he dispatch'd?

Murderer   My lord, his throat is cut; that I did for him.

Macbeth   Thou art the best o' the cut-throats! Yet he's good
That did the like for Fleance. If thou didst it,
²⁶ *Unparalleled, i.e. the best*
Thou art the nonpareil.²⁶   20

Murderer   Most royal sir,
Fleance is 'scaped.

Macbeth

[Aside] Then comes my fit again. I had else been
    perfect,
Whole as the marble, founded as the rock,
As broad and general as the casing²⁷ air;   25
But now I am cabin'd, cribb'd, confin'd,²⁸ bound in
To saucy doubts and fears. But Banquo's safe?

²⁷ *Surrounding*
²⁸ *Trapped*

Murderer

Ay, my good lord. Safe in a ditch he bides,
With twenty trenched²⁹ gashes on his head,
The least a death to nature.   30

²⁹ *Deep*

Macbeth

Thanks for that.
There the grown serpent lies; the worm³⁰ that's fled
Hath nature that in time will venom³¹ breed,
No teeth for the present. Get thee gone. Tomorrow
We'll hear ourselves again.   35

³⁰ *Snakelet*
³¹ *Poison*

Exit Murderer

Lady Macbeth

My royal lord,
You do not give the cheer. The feast is sold
That is not often vouch'd, while 'tis amaking,
'Tis given with welcome. To feed were best at home;
From thence the sauce to meat is ceremony;   40
Meeting were bare without it.

*Lady Macbeth is a gracious
hostess, reminding her husband
that the pomp and ceremony (the
sauce) of such a banquet adds to
the enjoyment of the meal*

Macbeth

Sweet remembrancer!³²
Now good digestion wait on appetite,
And health on both!

³² *Reminder*

Lennox

May't please your Highness sit.   45

The Ghost of Banquo enters and sits in Macbeth's place

Macbeth

Here had we now our country's honour roof'd,
Were the grac'd person of our Banquo present,
Who may I rather challenge for unkindness
Than pity for mischance.³³

³³ *Bad luck*

Ross	His absence, sir, 50 Lays blame upon his promise. Please't your Highness To grace us with your royal company?
Macbeth	The table's full.
Lennox	Here is a place reserv'd, sir.
Macbeth	Where? 55
Lennox	Here, my good lord. What is't that moves[34] your Highness?
Macbeth	Which of you have done this?
Lords	What, my good lord?
Macbeth	Thou canst not say I did it; never shake Thy gory[35] locks at me. 60
Ross	Gentlemen, rise; his Highness is not well.
Lady Macbeth	Sit, worthy friends; my lord is often thus, And hath been from his youth. Pray you, keep seat. The fit is momentary; upon a thought He will again be well. If much you note him, 65 You shall offend him and extend his passion. Feed, and regard him not. Are you a man?
Macbeth	Ay, and a bold one, that dare look on that Which might appall the devil.
Lady Macbeth	O proper stuff! 70 This is the very painting of your fear; This is the air-drawn dagger which you said Led you to Duncan. O, these flaws and starts, Impostors to true fear, would well become A woman's story at a winter's fire, 75 Authoris'd by her grandam.[36] Shame itself! Why do you make such faces? When all's done,

34 *Frightens, startles*

35 *Bloody*

36 *Grandmother*

You look but on a stool.

Macbeth Prithee, see there! Behold! Look! Lo! How say you?
Why, what care I? If thou canst nod, speak too. 80
If charnel houses[37] and our graves must send
Those that we bury back, our monuments
Shall be the maws[38] of kites.[39]

Exit Ghost

Lady Macbeth What, quite unmann'd in folly?

Macbeth If I stand here, I saw him. 85

Lady Macbeth Fie, for shame!

Macbeth Blood hath been shed ere now, i' the olden time,
Ere humane statute purg'd the gentle weal,[40]
Ay, and since too, murders have been perform'd
Too terrible for the ear. The time has been, 90
That, when the brains were out, the man would die,
And there an end; but now they rise again,
With twenty mortal murders on their crowns,
And push us from our stools. This is more strange
Than such a murder is. 95

Lady Macbeth My worthy lord,
Your noble friends do lack you.[41]

Macbeth I do forget.
Do not muse at me, my most worthy friends.
I have a strange infirmity, which is nothing
To those that know me. Come, love and health to all; 100
Then I'll sit down. Give me some wine, fill full.
I drink to the general joy o' the whole table,
And to our dear friend Banquo, whom we miss.
Would he were here! To all and him we thirst, 105
And all to all.

[37] *House of death, morgue*

[38] *Jaws* [39] *A kite is a large bird of prey*

[40] *Bruise*

[41] *Your friends are wondering where you are*

Macbeth is actually drawing attention to himself by constantly mentioning Banquo

Lords Our duties and the pledge.

Re-enter Ghost

Macbeth Avaunt,[42] and quit my sight! Let the earth hide thee!
Thy bones are marrowless, thy blood is cold;
Thou hast no speculation[43] in those eyes   110
Which thou dost glare with!

Lady Macbeth Think of this, good peers,
But as a thing of custom. 'Tis no other,
Only it spoils the pleasure of the time.

Macbeth What man dare, I dare.   115
Approach thou like the rugged Russian bear,
The arm'd rhinoceros, or the Hyrcan[44] tiger;
Take any shape but that, and my firm nerves
Shall never tremble. Or be alive again,
And dare me to the desert with thy sword.   120
If trembling I inhabit then, protest me
The baby of a girl. Hence, horrible shadow!
Unreal mockery, hence!

Exit Ghost

Why, so, being gone,
I am a man again. Pray you sit still.   125

Lady Macbeth You have displaced the mirth, broke the good
   meeting,
With most admir'd disorder.[45]

Macbeth Can such things be,
And overcome us like a summer's cloud,
Without our special wonder? You make me strange   130
Even to the disposition that I owe
When now I think you can behold such sights
And keep the natural ruby of your cheeks
When mine is blanch'd[46] with fear.

42 *Get away, leave*

43 *Life*

44 *Hyrcania, probably a Bengal tiger*

45 *Astonishing behaviour*

46 *Pale*

Ross	What sights, my lord?	135

Lady Macbeth   I pray you, speak not; he grows worse and worse;
Question enrages him. At once, good night.
Stand not upon the order of your going,
But go at once.

Lennox   Good night, and better health   140
Attend his Majesty!

Lady Macbeth   A kind good night to all!

Exit all but Macbeth and Lady Macbeth

Macbeth   It will have blood, they say; blood will have blood.
Stones have been known to move and trees to speak;
Augures and understood relations have   145
By maggot pies and choughs[47] and rooks brought forth
The secret'st man of blood. What is the night?

Lady Macbeth   Almost at odds with morning, which is which.

Macbeth   How say'st thou, that Macduff denies his person
At our great bidding?   150

Lady Macbeth   Did you send to him, sir?

Macbeth   I hear it by the way, but I will send.
There's not a one of them but in his house
I keep a servant fee'd. I will tomorrow,
And betimes I will, to the weird sisters.   155
More shall they speak; for now I am bent to know,
By the worst means, the worst. For mine own good
All causes shall give way. I am in blood
Stepp'd in so far that, should I wade no more,
Returning were as tedious as go o'er.   160
Strange things I have in head that will to hand,
Which must be acted ere they may be scann'd.

[47] *Crows*

Lady Macbeth	You lack the season of all natures, sleep.
Macbeth	Come, we'll to sleep. My strange and self-abuse
	Is the initiate fear that wants hard use. 165
	We are yet but young in deed.

Exit

MODERN ENGLISH VERSION

A HALL IN THE PALACE. A BANQUET PREPARED

Enter Macbeth, Lady Macbeth, Ross, Lennox, Lords, and Attendants

Macbeth	Welcome, everyone. You all know where to sit.
Lords	Thanks to your Majesty.
Macbeth	I'll have a chat with you all, and Lady Macbeth will join us.
Lady Macbeth	Everyone is welcome tonight.

Enter First Murderer to the door

Macbeth	We'll all laugh and be merry tonight!

Goes over to Murderer

Macbeth	There's blood on your face!
Murderer	Yeah, that's Banquo's.
Macbeth	Well, I'd prefer it on your face than in his body!
Murderer	I slashed his throat for him.

Macbeth	You're the best of the killers, although whoever killed Fleance is even better, and if you killed them both, then you're the best of all!
Murderer	Eh, sorry, but, eh, Fleance actually escaped.
Macbeth	Oh, no, I thought I could finally relax. Not now! But Banquo is definitely dead, is he?
Murderer	Oh, yeah. He's lying in a ditch. We stabbed him twenty times in the head. Even once would have killed him.
Macbeth	Well, thanks for that anyway. I'm glad Banquo is dead, but I wish Fleance was, too. Otherwise the Witches' prophecy could still come true.
	Exit Murderer
Lady Macbeth	You need to entertain our guests more, love. Food is only one part of the meal; socialising with your friends is the important thing.
Macbeth	Thanks for reminding me. Eat up, everyone. Let's enjoy ourselves!
	The Ghost of Banquo enters and sits in Macbeth's place
	It's great to have you all here, although there's no sign of Banquo. He must have been held up.
Ross	Well, he did promise he would be here, so I hope he keeps his word.
Macbeth	Hey, there's no seat for me!
Lennox	But your seat is empty and waiting for you.
Macbeth	Where?

Lennox	Here, my good lord. What's wrong?
Macbeth	Which of you has done this?
Lords	What, my good lord?
Macbeth	You cannot say I killed you! I didn't lay a finger on you! Don't shake your bloody hair at me!
Lady Macbeth	Don't mind my husband, he's just acting strangely. He has always been a bit eccentric, but that's why we love him. *[Whispers]* Get a grip!
Macbeth	Oh, God, even the devil would find it hard to look at your face; it's such a mess!
Lady Macbeth	*[Whispers]* Get a grip! You're looking at a stool! You're imagining things again, like when you thought you saw that dagger. You're talking to an empty stool. Everyone will think you're nuts.
Macbeth	Why are you staring at me? Go away!
Lady Macbeth	You're acting like a big girl.
	Exit Ghost
Macbeth	I know what I saw, and he was here!
Lady Macbeth	What the hell are you talking about?
Macbeth	It's so weird; dead people should not be able to come back among the living. I thought dead meant dead, but he came back!
Lady Macbeth	Everyone is looking at you.
Macbeth	Don't mind me, lads! I sometimes have these funny turns. Nothing to worry about. Had them since I was a kid. Let's get

back to enjoying our evening.

Lords Here's to the king!

Re-enter Ghost

Macbeth Get lost! Get out of my sight! Your body is drained of blood. Your eyes are empty! Get back into your grave!

Lady Macbeth Ignore him everyone, he's being silly.

Macbeth I would not be scared of anything or anyone else, but I cannot bear to see his face.

Exit Ghost

Phew! He's gone! I'm myself again.

Lady Macbeth You've ruined the whole evening.

Macbeth How could you all see what I saw and look so normal? You all have rosy cheeks, but I'm as pale as could be.

Ross What did you see?

Lady Macbeth Don't encourage him. In fact, let's call it a night. My husband is clearly not well.

Lennox Good night. I hope you feel better soon.

Lady Macbeth Good night, everyone.

Exit all but Macbeth and Lady Macbeth

Macbeth Blood will have blood. You cannot get away with murder. You'll pay the price eventually. What time is it?

Lady Macbeth Late.

Macbeth	Why wasn't Macduff here tonight? The cheek of him.
Lady Macbeth	Will you summon him?
Macbeth	Yes. Anyway, I find out everything, I have a spy in every household. And I'm going to find the Witches, and find out what else they know about my future. I'm up to my neck in blood. There's no going back so I'll have to keep going forward. More blood will have to be shed.
Lady Macbeth	You're tired. You don't know what you're saying. Let's go to bed.
Macbeth	Yes, let's go to sleep. I have only just begun.
	Exit

A HEATH. THUNDER

Enter the three Witches, meeting Hecate

First Witch   Why, how now, Hecate? You look angerly.

Hecate   Have I not reason, beldams[48] as you are,
Saucy and overbold? How did you dare
To trade and traffic with Macbeth
In riddles and affairs of death;   5
And I, the mistress of your charms,
The close contriver of all harms,
Was never call'd to bear my part,
Or show the glory of our art?
And, which is worse, all you have done   10
Hath been but for a wayward son,
Spiteful and wrathful, who, as others do,
Loves for his own ends, not for you.
But make amends now. Get you gone,
And at the pit of Acheron[49]   15
Meet me i' the morning. Thither he
Will come to know his destiny.
Your vessels and your spells provide,
Your charms and everything beside.
I am for the air; this night I'll spend   20
Unto a dismal and a fatal end.
Great business must be wrought ere noon:
Upon the corner of the moon
There hangs a vap'rous drop profound;
I'll catch it ere it come to ground.   25
And that distill'd by magic sleights
Shall raise such artificial sprites
As by the strength of their illusion
Shall draw him on to his confusion.
He shall spurn fate, scorn death, and bear   30
His hopes 'bove wisdom, grace, and fear.
And you all know security
Is mortals' chiefest enemy.

[48] *Ugly old woman – from the French 'belles dames' (beautiful women). Hecate is clearly being sarcastic*

[49] *Acheron was known as the river of pain in ancient Greek mythology*

Music and a song within, 'Come away, come away'

Hark! I am call'd; my little spirit, see,
Sits in a foggy cloud and stays for me.   35

Exit

First Witch   Come, let's make haste; she'll soon be back again.

Exit

THIS SCENE IS very different in style from the rest of *Macbeth*, and a new character is introduced, Hecate, whose name has already been mentioned several times by Macbeth. The Witches always speak in rhyming couplets, and so Hecate does, too. This serves to differentiate the Witches' dialogue from that of other characters, but also to give their words the quality of a chant or spell.

The Witches are quite clear in their aims and intentions, in a way that the other characters are not. There is no ambiguity about them; they are evil through and through. Shakespeare seems to have constructed the scenes involving the Witches with particular care. This may be because the audience response to them was so positive, because they add so much suspense and intrigue to the play. The Witches would also have been a source of interest to King James I, who had a particular fascination with witchcraft. Another

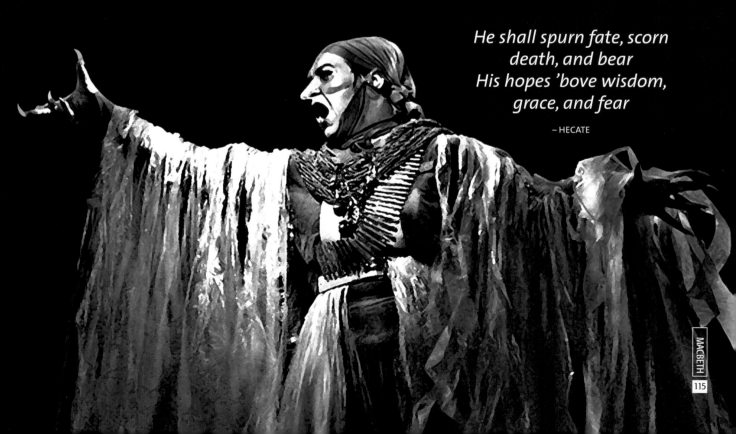

He shall spurn fate, scorn death, and bear His hopes 'bove wisdom, grace, and fear

– HECATE

reason may be that Shakespeare simply enjoyed creating these scenes and spent a long time perfecting them.

Hecate, the goddess of Witchcraft, chides the Witches for their involvement in Macbeth's affairs: *And I, the mistress of your charms, / The close contriver of all harms, / Was never call'd to bear my part, / Or show the glory of our art?* Hecate doesn't consider Macbeth worthy of their attention: *which is worse, all you have done / Hath been but for a wayward son, / Spiteful and wrathful, who, as others do, / Loves for his own ends, not for you.* What does Hecate mean by this? She says that Macbeth does not love the Witches – but who would love such creatures? What Hecate probably means is that Macbeth does not love evil for its own sake, but uses evil to satisfy his ambition. This may have been true at one point, but as the play progresses Macbeth certainly seems to be 'falling in love' with evil.

Hecate feels that the Witches have not gone far enough in involving themselves in Macbeth's affairs. Considering the appalling events that have transpired thus far, this seems a shocking thing to say. Hecate resolves to use her powers to affect Macbeth's fate. She will create 'spirits' (apparitions) to confuse and mislead him, and ultimately to bring about his destruction. This is enough to make the audience extremely apprehensive about what is to come.

[I] shall raise such artificial sprites
As by the strength of their illusion
Shall draw him on to his confusion.
He shall spurn fate, scorn death, and bear
His hopes 'bove wisdom, grace, and fear.
And you all know security
Is mortals' chiefest enemy.

A director can interpret this scene very dramatically. A monotonous drumbeat might be used to accompany Hecate's chants, and eerie lighting, dry ice and grotesque images can all contribute to its effect. This scene draws an eventful act towards its conclusion.

KEY **POINT**

- *Hecate is now involved in the Witches' diabolical scheming. As she is the most powerful Witch of all, this tells us that events far worse than any we have seen are about to happen.*

FORRES. THE PALACE

Enter Lennox and another Lord

Lennox   My former speeches have but hit your thoughts,
Which can interpret farther; only I say
Thing's have been strangely borne. The gracious Duncan
Was pitied of Macbeth; marry; he was dead.
And the right valiant Banquo walk'd too late,   5
Whom, you may say, if 't please you, Fleance kill'd,
For Fleance fled. Men must not walk too late.
Who cannot want the thought, how monstrous
It was for Malcolm and for Donalbain
To kill their gracious father? Damned fact!   10
How it did grieve Macbeth! Did he not straight,
In pious rage, the two delinquents tear
That were the slaves of drink and thralls of sleep?
Was not that nobly done? Ay, and wisely too,
For 'twould have anger'd any heart alive   15
To hear the men deny 't. So that, I say,
He has borne all things well; and I do think
That, had he Duncan's sons under his key –
As, an't please Heaven, he shall not – they should find
What 'twere to kill a father; so should Fleance.   20
But, peace! For from broad words, and 'cause he fail'd
His presence at the tyrant's feast, I hear,
Macduff lives in disgrace. Sir, can you tell
Where he bestows himself?

Lord   The son of Duncan,[50]   25
From whom this tyrant holds the due of birth,
Lives in the English court and is receiv'd
Of the most pious Edward[51] with such grace
That the malevolence of Fortune nothing
Takes from his high respect. Thither Macduff   30
Is gone to pray the holy King, upon his aid
To wake Northumberland and warlike Siward;[52]
That by the help of these, with Him above
To ratify the work, we may again

A tyrant is a cruel and oppressive ruler. Macbeth is increasingly referred to as a tyrant, meaning all of Scotland is suffering under his reign

[50] *Malcolm*

[51] *Edward the Confessor, an esteemed King of England in the 11th century AD*

[52] *A legendary English warrior. There are two Siwards in the play, father (Old Siward) and son (Young Siward)*

MACBETH

117

Give to our tables meat, sleep to our nights,   35
Free from our feasts and banquets bloody knives,
Do faithful homage, and receive free honours –
All which we pine for now. And this report
Hath so exasperate the King that he
Prepares for some attempt of war.   40

Lennox   Sent he to Macduff?

Lord   He did, and with an absolute 'Sir, not I,'
The cloudy messenger turns me his back,
And hums, as who should say, 'You'll rue[53] the time
That clogs me with this answer.'   45

Lennox   And that well might
Advise him to a caution, to hold what distance
His wisdom can provide. Some holy angel
Fly to the court of England and unfold
His message ere he come, that a swift blessing   50
May soon return to this our suffering country
Under a hand accurs'd!

Lord   I'll send my prayers with him.

Exit

[53] *Regret*

THIS SCENE SHOWS that after Macbeth's bizarre behaviour at the banquet and his crucial mistake in killing the Grooms, his crimes are now general knowledge. Lennox (another Scottish noble) speaks in a very sarcastic fashion, but does not directly say what he knows to be true. This is no doubt due to the spies that we know Macbeth has placed everywhere. So, with Lennox, it is not just what he says, but how he says it. Always remember that *Macbeth* is a play. The words on the page are really only part of the story. The actors' faces, gestures and tone of voice are essential parts of telling this story.

At first Lennox is circumspect and taciturn:

The gracious Duncan

Was pitied of Macbeth; marry, he was dead.

And the right valiant Banquo walk'd too late,

Whom, you may say, if 't please you, Fleance kill'd,

For Fleance fled.

But, no doubt encouraged by the obvious agreement of the lord with whom he is talking (who refers to Macbeth as a tyrant), he becomes blunter as the scene progresses: *that a swift blessing / May soon return to this our suffering country / Under a hand accurs'd!* This reminds us that the entire country is suffering with Macbeth as king.

The purpose of this scene is to fill us in on what is happening elsewhere. We learn that Macduff has angered Macbeth: *For from broad words, and 'cause he fail'd / His presence at the tyrant's feast, I hear, / Macduff lives in disgrace.* Malcolm, meanwhile, has received a warm welcome in England, and the English King Edward may send aid.

England, Scotland and Wales were separate realms in the period in which Macbeth is set. Each country had its own king and queen and its own rules and customs. But like all neighbouring countries, there was often a great deal of competition between them. Shakespeare's English audience would have loved the fact that it is one of their past kings, Edward the Confessor, who is coming to the rescue.

KEY **POINTS**

- *The Scottish lords are turning against Macbeth.*

- *Macduff has gone to England to ask for help to depose Macbeth.*

- *Malcolm has received safe haven at the court of Edward I.*

FOCUS ON ACT 3

'In some ways, this killing is worse than the murder of Duncan. Banquo is Macbeth's friend and a fellow soldier'

A
S ACT III BEGINS, it would be easy to assume that the high level of suspense created in Act II would be difficult to maintain and impossible to surpass. However, this act manages to be just as gripping, and arguably more unsettling, than Acts I and II. The murder of the two Grooms was the first indication that Macbeth was becoming dangerously unhinged. In this act, we see his paranoia grow and consume him. Macbeth is now King of Scotland, so the theme of kingship will be further explored, but in a different way. Previously, the theme was explored in Duncan's exceptionally good character. Now we will see what happens when a ruthless tyrant is on the throne.

At the close of Act II, we were left wondering if Banquo knew what Macbeth had done. In the first few lines of Act III, our questions are answered. Banquo does know that Macbeth is the real murderer, yet he says nothing: ***Thou hast it now: King, Cawdor, Glamis, all, / As the weird women promis'd; and, I fear, / Thou play'dst most foully for't.*** Knowing this, his silence is tantamount to treason.

When Macbeth invites him to a celebratory banquet that evening, Banquo promises to be there, unaware that Macbeth has hired assassins (representing the very worst of society, a far cry from the company Macbeth expected to be consorting with as king) to kill him and his son, Fleance. Macbeth probably knows that Banquo suspects him, but the Witches' prophecy, that Banquo's descendants will inherit the throne, is his main motive. He tries to justify the murder: ***To be thus is nothing; / But to be safely thus. Our fears in Banquo / Stick deep.***

In some ways, this killing is worse than the murder of

*Thou canst not say I did it; never shake
Thy gory locks at me*

– MACBETH (ACT III SCENE IV)

Duncan. Banquo is Macbeth's friend and a fellow soldier. Their relationship on the battlefield depended on having absolute trust in each other. Alliances forged in such a way were considered a sacred bond. It is a truly atrocious murder, somehow made worse by the fact that Macbeth gets others to do his dirty work.

Lady Macbeth's tough facade is now beginning to disintegrate. ***Nought's had, all's spent, / Where our desire is got without content***, she says, meaning that it was pointless killing Duncan if Macbeth is still not satisfied. She is no longer the equal partner we saw in Act I. Macbeth starts to exclude her from his plans and does not tell her he has arranged for Banquo and Fleance to be murdered: ***Be innocent of the knowledge*** … ***Till thou applaud the deed.*** Lady Macbeth is agitated and clearly unhappy. The burden of her guilty conscience weighs heavily upon her. And her husband's envy of Duncan has not diminished with the latter's death; if anything, it has grown deeper:

> ***Duncan is in his grave;***
> ***After life's fitful fever he sleeps well.***
> ***Treason has done his worst; nor steel, nor poison,***
> ***Malice domestic, foreign levy, nothing,***
> ***Can touch him further.***

Nothing can hurt Duncan any more. He sleeps peacefully, the kind of innocent sleep that Macbeth will never know again.

Banquo and Fleance are ambushed, and Banquo is brutally killed by ***twenty trenched gashes on his head; / The least a death to nature.*** Fleance escapes, however, and when Macbeth hears this he is enraged: ***the worm that's fled / Hath nature that in time will venom breed, / No***

teeth for the present.

Banquo had given his word to attend the banquet, but at the banquet that evening Macbeth instead sees Banquo's bloodied Ghost. His horror almost gives the game away: ***never shake / Thy gory locks at me.*** No one else sees Banquo, and so his Ghost might be said to be a manifestation of Macbeth's guilt. Lady Macbeth tries to cover for him, showing her continuing loyalty: ***Pray you, keep seat. / The fit is momentary; upon a thought / He will again be well.*** But eventually the guests must leave. To treat guests in this way would have been considered highly scandalous at this time. All those present now ask questions about Macbeth's demeanour, and inevitably they will all come to the obvious

A CAVERN. IN THE MIDDLE, A BOILING CAULDRON. THUNDER

Enter the three Witches

First Witch	Thrice the brindled[1] cat hath mew'd.
Second Witch	Thrice and once the hedge-pig whin'd.
Third Witch	Harpier cries, ''Tis time, 'tis time.'
First Witch	Round about the cauldron go;
	In the poison'd entrails[2] throw. 5
	Toad, that under cold stone
	Days and nights has thirty-one
	Swelter'd venom sleeping got,
	Boil thou first i' the charmed pot.
All	Double, double, toil and trouble; 10
	Fire burn and cauldron bubble.
Second Witch	Fillet of a fenny snake,[3]
	In the cauldron boil and bake;
	Eye of newt and toe of frog,
	Wool of bat and tongue of dog, 15
	Adder's fork and blind-worm's sting,
	Lizard's leg and howlet's[4] wing,
	For a charm of pow'rful trouble,
	Like a hell-broth boil and bubble.
All	Double, double, toil and trouble; 20
	Fire burn and cauldron bubble.
Third Witch	Scale of dragon, tooth of wolf,
	Witches' mummy, maw[5] and gulf[6]
	Of the ravin'd salt-sea shark,
	Root of hemlock[7] digg'd i' the dark, 25
	Liver of blaspheming Jew,
	Gall of goat and slips of yew[8]
	Silver'd in the moon's eclipse,

[1] *Striped*

The Witches each have a 'familiar', an animal who does their bidding. The third Witch's familiar is an owl called Harpier

[2] *Guts*

[3] *A snake found in the fen (marsh)*

[4] *Owlet (baby owl)*

[5] *Throat* [6] *Bosom*

[7] *Hemlock is a powerful poison*

[8] *Yew trees were often found in graveyards, and their leaves were thought to be nourished by the corpses buried there*

MACBETH

127

⁹ *Asian*

A particularly horrific ingredient, the finger of a baby, born to a prostitute in a ditch, and stillborn or killed at birth

¹⁰ *Prostitute*

¹¹ *Entrails*

Nose of Turk and Tartar's⁹ lips,
Finger of birth-strangled babe   30
Ditch-deliver'd by a drab,¹⁰
Make the gruel thick and slab.
Add thereto a tiger's chawdron,¹¹
For the ingredients of our cauldron.

All　　　　Double, double, toil and trouble;   35
Fire burn and cauldron bubble.

Second Witch　　Cool it with a baboon's blood,
Then the charm is firm and good.

Enter Hecate

Hecate　　O, well done! I commend your pains,
And everyone shall share i' the gains.   40
And now about the cauldron sing,
Like elves and fairies in a ring,
Enchanting all that you put in.

Music and a song, 'Black Spirits'. Hecate retires

Second Witch　　By the pricking of my thumbs,
Something wicked this way comes.   45
Open, locks,
Whoever knocks!

Enter Macbeth

Macbeth　　How now, you secret, black, and midnight hags!
What is't you do?

All　　　　A deed without a name.   50

Macbeth　　I conjure you, by that which you profess,
However you come to know it, answer me:
Though you untie the winds and let them fight
Against the churches, though the yesty¹² waves

¹² *Frothy*

Confound and swallow navigation up, 55
Though bladed corn be lodg'd and trees blown down,
Though castles topple on their warders' heads,
Though palaces and pyramids do slope
Their heads to their foundations, though the treasure
Of nature's germens[13] tumble all together 60
Even till destruction sicken, answer me
To what I ask you.

First Witch   Speak.

Second Witch   Demand.

Third Witch   We'll answer. 65

First Witch   Say, if thou'dst rather hear it from our mouths,
Or from our masters?

Macbeth   Call 'em, let me see 'em.

First Witch   Pour in sow's blood that hath eaten
Her nine farrow; grease that's sweaten 70
From the murderer's gibbet throw
Into the flame.

All   Come, high or low;
Thyself and office deftly show!

Thunder. First Apparition: an armed Head [14]

Macbeth   Tell me, thou unknown power – 75

First Witch   He knows thy thought:
Hear his speech, but say thou nought.

First Apparition   Macbeth! Macbeth! Macbeth! Beware Macduff,
Beware the Thane of Fife. Dismiss me. Enough.

Descends

[13] *Parts, meaning that all of nature's elements will get mixed up and confused*

The Witches pour in the blood of a sow that has eaten all of her piglets. They also add in the fat that drips from dead bodies left to hang on the gallows

[14] *A head wearing a helmet*

MACBETH

129

¹⁵ *Pricked*

¹⁶ *Powerful*

Macbeth	Whate'er thou art, for thy good caution, thanks; Thou hast harp'd¹⁵ my fear aright. But one word more –	80

Macbeth   Whate'er thou art, for thy good caution, thanks;   80
Thou hast harp'd¹⁵ my fear aright. But one word more –

First Witch   He will not be commanded. Here's another,
More potent¹⁶ than the first.

Thunder. Second Apparition: a bloody Child

Second Apparition   Macbeth! Macbeth! Macbeth!

Macbeth   Had I three ears, I'd hear thee.   85

Second Apparition   Be bloody, bold, and resolute: laugh to scorn
The power of man, for none of woman born
Shall harm Macbeth.

Descends

Macbeth   Then live, Macduff. What need I fear of thee?
But yet I'll make assurance double sure,   90
And take a bond of fate: thou shalt not live,
That I may tell pale-hearted fear it lies,
And sleep in spite of thunder.

***Thunder. Third Apparition: a Child crowned,
with a tree in his hand***

What is this,
That rises like the issue of a king,   95
And wears upon his baby brow the round
And top of sovereignty?

All   Listen, but speak not to't.

Third Apparition   Be lion-mettled, proud, and take no care
Who chafes, who frets, or where conspirers are.   100
Macbeth shall never vanquish'd be until
Great Birnam Wood to high Dunsinane Hill
Shall come against him.

I am in this earthly world, where to do harm
Is often laudable, to do good sometime
Accounted dangerous folly

– LADY MACDUFF

MODERN ENGLISH VERSION

FIFE. MACDUFF'S CASTLE

Enter Lady Macduff, her Son, and Ross

Lady Macduff   Why has he run away? Did he do something wrong?

Ross   You just have to be patient.

Lady Macduff   He had none! He was mad to run, just because he was afraid.

Ross   You don't know whether it was his wisdom or his fear.

Lady Macduff   Wisdom? To leave his wife, to leave his babies, to leave his house, and to leave all his things behind? He mustn't love us. If Scotland is so bad, then why didn't he stay to protect us? Even a little wren will fight to the death to protect her nest.

Ross   I cannot really explain much, or I could get us both into trouble. But your husband is not a coward. He is brave and noble, really. I know things seem bleak at the moment, but they'll surely get better.

Lady Macduff   My son has a father, and yet he is fatherless, because my husband has left us.

Ross   I have to go. I don't want to get myself in trouble or put you in an awkward position.

Leaves

Lady Macduff   Well, son, your father's gone. How will we survive without him?

Son   As birds do, Mum.

Lady Macduff   What, with worms and flies?

Son   They just take it day by day, and so will we.

Lady Macduff	Birds can be trapped and killed.
Son	Not necessarily, Mum. And Dad isn't necessarily dead either.
Lady Macduff	Yes, he is dead. What will you do without a father?
Son	No, what will you do for a husband?
Lady Macduff	I can get twenty husbands in the market.
Son	And you can sell them back to the market when you're finished with them!
Lady Macduff	Oh, you little chancer!
Son	Was Dad a traitor?
Lady Macduff	Yes.
Son	What is a traitor?
Lady Macduff	A traitor is someone who breaks his promises.
Son	So anyone who breaks a promise is a traitor?
Lady Macduff	Exactly, and they should be hanged.
Son	All of them?
Lady Macduff	Every one of them.
Son	Who should do the hanging?
Lady Macduff	The non-traitors, all the honest people!
Son	That won't happen, Mum. There are so many liars and traitors, they'd outnumber the honest people, and hang them.
Lady Macduff	Very funny – but you still need a new Dad.

Son	If you really thought he was dead, you'd be crying for him. Or maybe it'd mean I was getting a new father.
Lady Macduff	You're too cheeky!

Enter a Messenger

Messenger	I'm really sorry to disturb you, I know I'm a stranger, but I have to warn you to get away from this place fast. If you stay here, something awful is going to happen to you and your children. Please believe me, and leave immediately!

Exit

Lady Macduff	What? Where the hell should I go? I haven't done anything wrong. But I guess that doesn't mean anything in the world we live in today. It is often the good people who suffer and the bad people who are rewarded.

Enter Murderers

First Murderer	Where is your husband?
Lady Macduff	I don't know. But even if I did, I would not tell someone like you.
First Murderer	He's a traitor.
Son	You're a liar!
First Murderer	You're just like your traitor of a father.

Stabs him

Son	I'm dying, Mum. Save yourself! Run!

Dies

Exit Lady Macduff crying, 'Murder!'
Exit Murderers, following her

ENGLAND. BEFORE THE KING'S PALACE

Enter Malcolm and Macduff

Malcolm Let us seek out some desolate shade and there
Weep our sad bosoms empty.

Macduff Let us rather
Hold fast the mortal sword, and like good men
Bestride[25] our downfall'n birthdom. Each new morn   5
New widows howl, new orphans cry, new sorrows
Strike heaven on the face, that it resounds
As if it felt with Scotland and yell'd out
Like syllable of dolour.[26]

Malcolm What I believe, I'll wail;   10
What know, believe; and what I can redress,
As I shall find the time to friend, I will.
What you have spoke, it may be so perchance.
This tyrant, whose sole name blisters our tongues,
Was once thought honest. You have loved him well;   15
He hath not touch'd you yet. I am young, but something
You may deserve of him through me, and wisdom
To offer up a weak, poor, innocent lamb
To appease an angry god.

Macduff I am not treacherous.   20

Malcolm But Macbeth is.
A good and virtuous nature may recoil
In an imperial charge.[27] But I shall crave your pardon;
That which you are, my thoughts cannot transpose.
Angels are bright still, though the brightest fell.   25
Though all things foul would wear the brows of grace,
Yet grace must still look so.

Macduff I have lost my hopes.

Malcolm Perchance even there where I did find my doubts.
Why in that rawness left you wife and child,[28]   30

25 *Get over*

26 *Sorrow, distress*

27 *Even a good person may commit evil deeds on a king's orders*

28 *He has left his wife and children vulnerable*

²⁹ *Suspicions*

Those precious motives, those strong knots of love,
Without leave-taking? I pray you,
Let not my jealousies²⁹ be your dishonours,
But mine own safeties. You may be rightly just,
Whatever I shall think.   35

Macduff

Bleed, bleed, poor country!
Great tyranny, lay thou thy basis sure,
For goodness dare not check thee. Wear thou thy wrongs;
The title is affeer'd. Fare thee well, lord.
I would not be the villain that thou think'st   40
For the whole space that's in the tyrant's grasp
And the rich East to boot.

*Malcolm does not yet trust Macduff,
but Macduff insists he would not be
on Macbeth's side for anything,
even all the riches of the East*

Malcolm

Be not offended;
I speak not as in absolute fear of you.
I think our country sinks beneath the yoke;   45
It weeps, it bleeds, and each new day a gash
Is added to her wounds. I think withal
There would be hands uplifted in my right;
And here from gracious England have I offer
Of goodly thousands.³⁰ But for all this,   50
When I shall tread upon the tyrant's head,
Or wear it on my sword, yet my poor country
Shall have more vices than it had before,
More suffer and more sundry ways than ever,
By him that shall succeed.   55

*A yoke was a type of harness made of
wood, placed on the necks of working
animals like oxen. It also means a
heavy burden. So Macbeth's reign has
burdened all of Scotland*

³⁰ *England has offered its own soldiers
to help in the fight against Macbeth*

Macduff

What should he be?

Malcolm

It is myself I mean, in whom I know
All the particulars of vice so grafted
That, when they shall be open'd, black Macbeth
Will seem as pure as snow, and the poor state   60
Esteem him as a lamb, being compar'd
With my confineless harms.³¹

*Malcolm is pretending to be
worse than Macbeth in order
to gauge Macduff's reaction*

³¹ *Infinite evil traits*

Macduff

Not in the legions
Of horrid hell can come a devil more damn'd

In evils to top Macbeth.

Malcolm I grant him bloody, 65
Luxurious,[32] avaricious,[33] false, deceitful,
Sudden, malicious, smacking of every sin
That has a name,[34] But there's no bottom, none,
In my voluptuousness.[35] Your wives, your daughters,
Your matrons, and your maids could not fill up 70
The cistern[36] of my lust, and my desire
All continent impediments would o'erbear[37]
That did oppose my will. Better Macbeth
Than such a one to reign.

Macduff Boundless intemperance[38] 75
In nature is a tyranny; it hath been
The untimely emptying of the happy throne,
And fall of many kings. But fear not yet
To take upon you what is yours. You may
Convey your pleasures in a spacious plenty 80
And yet seem cold, the time you may so hoodwink.[39]
We have willing dames enough; there cannot be
That vulture in you to devour so many
As will to greatness dedicate themselves,
Finding it so inclined. 85

Malcolm With this there grows
In my most ill-compos'd affection such
A stanchless avarice that, were I King,
I should cut off the nobles for their lands,
Desire his jewels and this other's house; 90
And my more-having would be as a sauce
To make me hunger more, that I should forge
Quarrels unjust against the good and loyal,
Destroying them for wealth.

Macduff This avarice 95
Sticks deeper, grows with more pernicious root
Than summer-seeming lust, and it hath been
The sword of our slain kings. Yet do not fear;

[32] *Lecherous* [33] *Greedy, corrupt*

[34] *Macbeth is guilty of every one of the seven deadly sins*

[35] *Desire for sex*

[36] *Reservoir*

[37] *Nothing could stop him*

[38] *No self-control*

[39] *Fool, deceive*

40 *Plenty*

Scotland hath foisons[40] to fill up your will
Of your mere own. All these are portable,   100
With other graces weigh'd.

Malcolm   But I have none. The king-becoming graces,
As justice, verity, temperance, stableness,
Bounty, perseverance, mercy, lowliness,
Devotion, patience, courage, fortitude,   105

41 *Love*

I have no relish[41] of them, but abound
In the division of each several crime,
Acting it many ways. Nay, had I power, I should

42 *Peace*

Pour the sweet milk of concord[42] into hell,
Uproar the universal peace, confound   110
All unity on earth.

Macduff   O Scotland, Scotland!

Malcolm   If such a one be fit to govern, speak.
I am as I have spoken.

Macduff   Fit to govern?   115
No, not to live. O nation miserable!

43 *Badly ruled*

With an untitled tyrant bloody-sceptre'd,[43]
When shalt thou see thy wholesome days again,
Since that the truest issue of thy throne

Macduff is devastated by Malcolm's pretence, especially as Duncan was such a great king, and Malcolm's mother a saintly woman who prayed and did penance every day of her life

44 *By his own admission*

By his own interdiction[44] stands accurs'd   120
And does blaspheme his breed? Thy royal father
Was a most sainted king; the queen that bore thee,
Oftener upon her knees than on her feet,
Died every day she lived. Fare thee well!
These evils thou repeat'st upon thyself   125
Have banish'd me from Scotland. O my breast,
Thy hope ends here!

Malcolm   Macduff, this noble passion,
Child of integrity, hath from my soul

45 *Doubts*

Wip'd the black scruples,[45] reconcil'd my thoughts   130
To thy good truth and honour. Devilish Macbeth
By many of these trains hath sought to win me

Malcolm   Be comforted.
                   Let's make us medicine of our great revenge,   250
                   To cure this deadly grief.

Macduff   He has no children. All my pretty ones?
                   Did you say all? O hell-kite! All?
                   What, all my pretty chickens and their dam[61]
                   At one fell swoop?   255

Malcolm   Dispute it like a man.

Macduff   I shall do so,
                   But I must also feel it as a man.
                   I cannot but remember such things were
                   That were most precious to me. Did Heaven look on,   260
                   And would not take their part? Sinful Macduff,
                   They were all struck for thee! Naught that I am,
                   Not for their own demerits,[62] but for mine,
                   Fell slaughter on their souls. Heaven rest them now!

Malcolm   Be this the whetstone[63] of your sword. Let grief   265
                   Convert to anger; blunt not the heart, enrage it.

Macduff   O, I could play the woman with mine eyes[64]
                   And braggart with my tongue![65] But, gentle heavens,
                   Cut short all intermission;[66] front to front
                   Bring thou this fiend of Scotland and myself;   270
                   Within my sword's length set him; if he 'scape,
                   Heaven forgive him too!

Malcolm   This tune goes manly.
                   Come, go we to the King; our power is ready;
                   Our lack is nothing but our leave. Macbeth   275
                   Is ripe for shaking, and the powers above
                   Put on their instruments. Receive what cheer you may;
                   The night is long that never finds the day.

                   Exit

[61] Mother

[62] Sins

[63] A whetstone was used to sharpen knives. Malcolm tells Macduff to use his hatred of Macbeth to destroy him

[64] This simply means that Macduff could cry, although it was considered unmanly to do so

[65] There is a lot Macduff could say about his tremendous loss

[66] Interruption

MACBETH

153

SCENE **ANALYSIS**

IN THIS SCENE, the action moves away from Macbeth and Scotland. This scene takes place in England, in front of King Edward's palace. Macduff has arrived there to plead for English assistance in deposing Macbeth. He paints Malcolm a vivid image of Scotland's distress: *Each new morn / New widows howl, new orphans cry, new sorrows / Strike heaven on the face.*

Malcolm is just a young man, but he is clearly his father's son. Duncan was exemplary in every way; the only criticism one could make of him was that he was too trusting. For that reason, it is impressive to see that Malcolm does not trust Macduff straight away and points out that, at one time, everyone trusted Macbeth: *What you have spoke, it may be so perchance. / This tyrant, whose sole name blisters our tongues, / Was once thought honest.* When Macduff protests his loyalty, Malcolm suggests that he has taken a great personal risk in fleeing Scotland: *Why in that rawness left you wife and child, / Those precious motives, those strong knots of love, / Without leave-taking?* These lines are another example of dramatic irony, because the audience is aware of the terrible fate that has been visited upon Macduff's unguarded family.

Malcolm proceeds to test Macduff's honour in a roundabout, even childish way, though it is effective. He says that he himself would make a terrible king; greedy, lusty, tyrannical, confrontational: *I should forge / Quarrels unjust against the good and loyal, / Destroying them for wealth.* Macduff refuses to swear loyalty to him and breaks down in tears at the thought of Scotland's future – *These evils thou*

repeat'st upon thyself / Have banish'd me from Scotland. At this, Malcolm can be confident that Macduff is loyal and steadfast. The two men agree to unite in order to defeat Macbeth.

The act concludes with Ross's arrival to break the terrible news to Macduff of his family's death. Macduff weeps out of sorrow and guilt, and his pain is so believable that it is natural for us to think that Shakespeare is recalling his own pain upon the death of his son, Hamnet. Shakespeare also left his family, not to save his country, but to pursue his theatrical career. He must have felt some guilt at this decision, and perhaps the playwright's own emotions help make Macduff's words so very poignant: *I must also feel it as a man. / I cannot but remember such things were / That were most precious to me.* Malcolm comforts Macduff and tells him to hold firm until the final confrontation with Macbeth, when he can take his revenge: *Let's make us medicine of our great revenge, / To cure this deadly grief.*

KEY **POINTS**

- *Malcolm shows his kingly ability in the way he tests Macduff's loyalty thoroughly before deciding to trust him.*

- *Macduff learns of his family's slaughter, and it utterly devastates him.*

- *Malcolm agrees to return to Scotland with Macduff to seize the throne from Macbeth.*

Let's make us medicine of our great revenge,
To cure this deadly grief

– MALCOLM

MACBETH

155

FOCUS ON ACT 4

'The murder of a
child marks
Macbeth's lowest
point in the play, and
is a richly symbolic
image of the depths
of evil to which he
has now sunk'

THIS ACT, which contains three incredibly dramatic scenes, moves the plot forward in preparation for the finale.

In Scene I, Macbeth seeks out the Witches, desperate for some answers about his future. This scene is often referred to as 'the cauldron scene'. The Witches do not answer his questions directly but concoct a terrible brew that causes four Apparitions to appear. The ingredients they throw into the cauldron include poisoned bowels, toad's sweat, a dog's tongue, a witch's corpse and, most appalling of all, the finger of a stillborn child born to a prostitute in a ditch. Hardly surprising, then, that the Apparitions which appear from the pot are so disturbing.

The Apparitions – a head wearing a helmet, a bloody child, a child wearing a crown, and an array of kings – lead Macbeth to believe that his position is unassailable, but that he must beware Macduff, and that the future of his line is still uncertain. In the end, they leave Macbeth as paranoid as before, and he resolves to do anything he wants to help secure his throne: *From this moment / The very firstlings of my heart shall be / The firstlings of my hand*.

And to begin, when Lennox informs Macbeth that Macduff has fled to England, he decides there and then to slaughter this unfaithful lord's family.

Scene II is a domestic one. We see Lady Macduff and her young son chatting affectionately:

Son	***Nay, how will you do for a husband?***
Lady Macduff	***Why, I can buy me twenty at any market.***
Son	***Then you'll buy 'em to sell again.***

The dramatic purpose of this scene is to act as a contrast to

DUNSINANE. ANTEROOM IN THE CASTLE

Enter a Doctor of Physic and a Waiting Gentlewoman

Doctor I have two nights watch'd with you, but can perceive no truth in your report. When was it she last walk'd?[1]

Gentlewoman Since his Majesty went into the field, I have seen her rise from her bed, throw her nightgown upon her, unlock her closet, take forth paper, fold it, 5 write upon 't, read it, afterwards seal it, and again return to bed; yet all this while in a most fast sleep.

Doctor A great perturbation[2] in nature, to receive at once the benefit of sleep and do the effects of watching! In this slumb'ry agitation,[3] besides her 10 walking and other actual performances, what, at any time, have you heard her say?

[2] *Disturbance or upheaval*

[3] *Disturbed sleep*

Gentlewoman That, sir, which I will not report after her.

Doctor You may to me, and 'tis most meet you should.

Gentlewoman Neither to you nor any one, having no witness to 15 confirm my speech.

Enter Lady Macbeth with a taper[4]

[4] *A candle*

Lo you, here she comes! This is her very guise,[5] and, upon my life, fast asleep. Observe her; stand close.

[5] *Appearance*

Doctor How came she by that light?

Gentlewoman Why, it stood by her. She has light by her continually; 'tis her command. 20

Doctor You see, her eyes are open.

Gentlewoman Ay, but their sense is shut.[6]

[6] *Lady Macbeth is fast asleep, even though her eyes are wide open*

Doctor   What is it she does now? Look how she rubs her hands.

Gentlewoman   It is an accustom'd action with her, to seem thus
washing her hands. I have known her continue in   25
this a quarter of an hour.

Lady Macbeth   Yet here's a spot.

Doctor   Hark, she speaks! I will set down what comes from her,
To satisfy my remembrance the more strongly.[7]

7 He will write down what she says, to help him remember

8 A spot of blood that she cannot wash away

Lady Macbeth   Out, damned spot! Out, I say![8] One – two – why then 'tis   30
time to do't. Hell is murky. Fie, my lord, fie! A soldier, and
afeard?[9] What need we fear who knows it, when none can
call our power to account? Yet who would have thought
the old man to have had so much blood in him?

9 Afraid

Lady Macbeth is haunted by Duncan's murder and her involvement in manipulating her husband. The line 'Out, damned spot!' is iconic because it demonstrates the permanence of guilt. It is a powerful visual spectacle to see Lady Macbeth furiously try to clean her hands of guilt

Doctor   Do you mark that?   35

10 Lady Macduff

Lady Macbeth   The Thane of Fife had a wife;[10] where is she now?
What, will these hands ne'er be clean? No more o' that,
my lord, no more o' that. You mar[11] all with this starting.

11 Ruin

Doctor   Go to, go to; you have known what you should not.

Gentlewoman   She has spoke what she should not, I am sure of that.   40
Heaven knows what she has known.

These lines show how very wrong Lady Macbeth was when she said, 'A little water clears us of this deed' after Duncan's murder in Act II

Lady Macbeth   Here's the smell of the blood still. All the perfumes of
Arabia will not sweeten this little hand. Oh, oh, oh!

12 Burdened

Doctor   What a sigh is there! The heart is sorely charged.[12]

Gentlewoman   I would not have such a heart in my bosom for the   45
dignity of the whole body.

Doctor   Well, well, well –

Gentlewoman   Pray God it be, sir.

Doctor   This disease is beyond my practice. Yet I have known
those who have walk'd in their sleep who have died   50
holily in their beds.

Lady Macbeth   Wash your hands, put on your nightgown; look not so
pale. I tell you yet again, Banquo's buried; he cannot
come out on's grave.

Doctor   Even so?

Lady Macbeth   To bed, to bed; there's knocking at the gate. Come,   55
come, come, come, give me your hand. What's done
cannot be undone. To bed, to bed, to bed.

Exit

Doctor   Will she go now to bed?

Gentlewoman   Directly.

Doctor   Foul whisperings are abroad. Unnatural deeds   60
Do breed unnatural troubles; infected minds
To their deaf pillows will discharge their secrets.
More needs she the divine than the physician.[13]
God, God, forgive us all! Look after her;
Remove from her the means of all annoyance,   65
And still keep eyes upon her. So good night.
My mind she has mated and amaz'd my sight.
I think, but dare not speak.

Gentlewoman   Good night, good doctor.

Exit

*Lady Macbeth is reliving the
night of Duncan's murder over
and over. She also feels
responsible for the deaths of
Banquo and Macduff's family*

[13] *Lady Macbeth needs a priest and
God's mercy, not a doctor*

*The Doctor fears that Lady
Macbeth will commit suicide*

THIS IS A crucial scene and notable for being different from any that has preceded it. Lady Macbeth has been absent from the play since Act III. This scene marks her last appearance in the play, and it is interesting to contrast it with her first. Originally, we thought Lady Macbeth was a monster. Shakespeare, however, gave some hints that this was not really the case – such as the way she needed to drink to bolster her courage, or how she could not kill Duncan because he looked like her father. Now we see a broken woman, haunted and tormented by what she has done. Her lady-in-waiting observes her night-time agitation:

> *Since his Majesty went into the field, I have seen her rise from her bed, throw her nightgown upon her, unlock her closet, take forth paper, fold it, write upon 't, read it, afterwards seal it, and again return to bed; yet all this while in a most fast sleep.*

In Shakespeare's day, sleepwalking was seen as the sign of a guilty conscience. It was also considered an indicator of deep distress.

The letter the lady-in-waiting mentions is the fateful letter Macbeth sent his wife in Act I, which was the catalyst for everything that happened subsequently. The lady-in-waiting also reports that *It is an accustom'd action with her, to seem thus washing her hands. I have known her continue in this a quarter of an hour.* After Duncan's murder, Lady Macbeth remarked that *A little water clears us of this deed*, but she has since discovered that guilt cannot be washed away. She scrubs pathetically at her hands – *Out, damned spot! Out, I say!* – but cannot wash off the metaphorical blood. This realisation leaves her desolate: *What, will these hands ne'er be clean?*

The Doctor listens, appalled, as Lady Macbeth seemingly confesses all. *The old man* with *so much blood in him* is Duncan. The Thane of Fife's wife is Lady Macduff. She also mentions Banquo: *Banquo's buried; he cannot come out on's grave*. Lady Macbeth feels guilty for these later murders because she recognises that Macbeth would not have committed them if she had not pushed him into murdering Duncan to begin with.

At the end of the scene, the Doctor advises the lady-in-waiting to keep a close eye on her mistress, because Lady Macbeth is a risk to herself and likely to attempt suicide: *Look after her; / Remove from her the means of all annoyance, / And still keep eyes upon her.*

This scene is intended to shock us with its contrast between the ferocious manipulator of Act I, Scene V and the pitiful woman we see here. It forces us to re-examine what we felt we knew about Lady Macbeth and re-evaluate what we thought about her character. The reaction of the audience most likely mirrors that of the Doctor: *My mind she has mated and amaz'd my sight.*

KEY **POINTS**

- *The theme of guilt is vividly brought to life through Lady Macbeth's distressed state.*

- *Lady Macbeth is not the monster we initially thought.*

- *The motif of blood is again used to symbolise guilt, but this time the blood is not actually there. The very non-existence of blood is what makes this scene so effective.*

THIS IS ONE of the few scenes where we get an insight into what is going on inside Macbeth's head. Despite all appearances to the contrary, he remains confident and defiant, putting his trust completely in the Witches' prophecies:

> *Bring me no more reports; let them fly all!*
> *Till Birnam Wood remove to Dunsinane*
> *I cannot taint with fear. What's the boy Malcolm?*
> *Was he not born of woman? The spirits that know*
> *All mortal consequences have pronounced me thus:*
> *'Fear not, Macbeth; no man that's born of woman*
> *Shall e'er have power upon thee.'*

Macbeth, however, seems somewhat jaded. He is beginning to realise all he has lost. He is getting old, *My way of life / is fall'n into the sear*, and whereas most people enjoy that part of their life with friends, children and grandchildren, he has none of those things *which should accompany old age, / As honour, love, obedience, troops of friends* … Instead, he is universally hated and feared. People may be too afraid to articulate their hatred, but he is painfully aware of how he is reviled.

Macbeth also has an interesting conversation with the Doctor, who informs him that Lady Macbeth's illness is emotional, not physical: *Not so sick, my lord, / As she is troubled with thick-coming fancies, / That keep her from her rest.* Macbeth asks if painful memories can be 'plucked' from the brain, and there is a sense, too, that he would like to forget what he has seen and what he has done. Yet, at the close of the scene he remains defiant: *I will not be afraid of death and bane / Till Birnam Forest come to Dunsinane.*

KEY **POINTS**

- *Macbeth realises that he has lost not only everything in his past but also any kind of future.*

- *Macbeth asks about his wife's health, but he does not seem overly concerned about her or indeed anything or anyone but himself.*

- *Macbeth still trusts the Witches' prophecies and continues to feel invincible as a result.*

COUNTRY NEAR BIRNAM WOOD. DRUM AND COLOURS

Enter Malcolm, old Seward and his Son, Macduff, Menteith, Caithness, Angus, Lennox, Ross, and Soldiers, marching

Malcolm   Cousins, I hope the days are near at hand
That chambers will be safe.

Menteith   We doubt it nothing.

Siward   What wood is this before us?

Menteith   The Wood of Birnam.   5

Malcolm   Let every soldier hew[42] him down a bough,[43]
And bear 't before him; thereby shall we shadow
The numbers of our host, and make discovery
Err in report of us.[44]

Soldiers   It shall be done.   10

Siward   We learn no other but the confident tyrant
Keeps still in Dunsinane and will endure
Our setting down before 't.

Malcolm   'Tis his main hope;
For where there is advantage to be given,   15
Both more and less have given him the revolt,[45]
And none serve with him but constrained[46] things
Whose hearts are absent too.

Macduff   Let our just censures[47]
Attend the true event, and put we on   20
Industrious soldiership.[48]

Siward   The time approaches
That will with due decision make us know
What we shall say we have and what we owe.
Thoughts speculative their unsure hopes relate,   25
But certain issue strokes must arbitrate.
Towards which advance the war.

Exit marching

Remember that the Witches told Macbeth he would not be vanquished until Birnam Wood moved to Dunsinane. Malcolm orders the soldiers to camouflage themselves with branches and advance on Dunsinane – hence the woods are moving

[42] Cut   [43] Branch

[44] Thus camouflaged, they can take Macbeth by surprise

[45] Most of Macbeth's men have fled

[46] Imprisoned, captive

[47] Disapproval

[48] Do their best as soldiers

MUCH OF THE action of Act V moves between Macbeth in the castle at Dunsinane and the English forces advancing on the ground. In this scene, we can see how like his father young Malcolm is and how he is maturing in readiness for the throne. He comes up with the ingenious idea of having the soldiers camouflage themselves: *Let every soldier hew him down a bough / And bear 't before him.*

This scene is also significant because it shows how sly and treacherous the Witches really are and how they have tricked Macbeth. He thought himself invincible, because how could an entire wood ever move? But Birnam Wood will appear to move as the camouflaged soldiers advance. The suspense increases as we wonder how Macbeth will react.

We also learn that no one remains loyal to Macbeth: *none serve with him but constrained things / Whose hearts are absent too.*

KEY **POINTS**

- *The woods are about to move. This will be Macbeth's first indication that he is not invincible.*

- *Malcolm is maturing and becoming more kingly in every scene.*

- *No one supports Macbeth any longer.*

DUNSINANE. WITHIN THE CASTLE

Enter Macbeth, Seyton, and Soldiers, with drum and colours

49 *Macbeth's royal crest*

Macbeth
Hang out our banners[49] on the outward walls;
The cry is still, 'They come!' Our castle's strength
Will laugh a siege to scorn. Here let them lie
Till famine and the ague[50] eat them up.
Were they not forc'd[51] with those that should be ours, 5
We might have met them dareful, beard to beard,[52]
And beat them backward home.

So many of Macbeth's soldiers have defected that he decides to stay put in the castle rather than meet the enemy on the battlefield

50 *Fever*
51 *Reinforced*
52 *Face to face*

A cry of women within

What is that noise?

Seyton
It is the cry of women, my good lord.

Exit

Macbeth
I have almost forgot the taste of fears: 10
The time has been, my senses would have cool'd
To hear a night-shriek, and my fell of hair
Would at a dismal treatise[53] rouse and stir[54]
As life were in 't. I have supp'd full with horrors;
Direness,[55] familiar to my slaughterous thoughts, 15
Cannot once start me.

53 *Scary story* 54 *His hair would stand on end*

55 *Horror*

Re-enter Seyton

Wherefore was that cry?

Seyton
The Queen, my lord, is dead.

56 *Later, i.e. her death is premature*

Macbeth
She should have died hereafter;[56]
There would have been a time for such a word. 20
Tomorrow, and tomorrow, and tomorrow
Creeps in this petty pace from day to day

To the last syllable of recorded time;
And all our yesterdays have lighted fools
The way to dusty death. Out, out, brief candle!   25
Life's but a walking shadow, a poor player
That struts and frets his hour upon the stage
And then is heard no more. It is a tale
Told by an idiot, full of sound and fury,
Signifying nothing.   30

Enter a Messenger

Thou comest to use thy tongue; thy story quickly.

Messenger   Gracious my lord,
I should report that which I say I saw,
But know not how to do it.

Macbeth   Well, say, sir.   35

Messenger   As I did stand my watch upon the hill,
I look'd toward Birnam, and anon, methought,
The wood began to move.

Macbeth   Liar and slave!

Messenger   Let me endure your wrath,[57] if 't be not so.   40
Within this three mile may you see it coming;
I say, a moving grove.

Macbeth   If thou speak'st false,
Upon the next tree shalt thou hang alive,
Till famine cling thee;[58] if thy speech be sooth,[59]   45
I care not if thou dost for me as much.
I pull in resolution and begin
To doubt the equivocation of the fiend[60]
That lies like truth. 'Fear not, till Birnam Wood
Do come to Dunsinane,' and now a wood   50
Comes toward Dunsinane. Arm, arm, and out!
If this which he avouches does appear,

This is one of the most important speeches in Shakespeare's entire body of work. It is a profound meditation on a wasted life. Macbeth says that life is as brief as a candle's flame and you only have one chance to get it right. This is as close as Macbeth comes to expressing regret and acknowledging that he has ruined his life

[57] *Anger*

[58] *Until he starves to death*   [59] *True*

[60] *Macbeth is beginning to see that the Witches have lied to him*

MACBETH

179

*Macbeth is tired of it all
and is ready for death*

There is nor flying hence nor tarrying here.
I 'gin to be aweary of the sun
And wish the estate o' the world were now undone.   55
Ring the alarum bell! Blow, wind! Come, wrack!
At least we'll die with harness on our back.

Exit

*She should have died hereafter;
There would have been a time
for such a word*

– MACBETH

WHILE THE AUDIENCE has known for a long time that the end is coming, this is really the first time that Macbeth realises it. He is preparing to defend the castle, still defiant, when two pieces of news appear to cause him to lose his resolve. The first is that Lady Macbeth is dead: ***The Queen, my lord, is dead.*** Apparently, she has committed suicide. The second is that a servant swears that Birnam Wood is starting to move towards Dunsinane: ***As I did stand my watch upon the hill, / I look'd toward Birnam, and anon, methought, / The wood began to move.***

These revelations are the catalyst for Macbeth to do some soul-searching, or as much soul-searching as he is capable of at this point. Shakespeare loves to use the theatre as a metaphor and does so here when he gives his character one of the most famous lines in literature: ***Life's but a walking shadow, a poor player / That struts and frets his hour upon the stage.*** Macbeth realises that he had one chance at life and he blew it. He speaks earlier on in the play about losing his ***eternal jewel*** (his soul) by murdering Duncan. Now he realises that life is brief, but the afterlife is forever. In Shakespeare's time, people firmly believed that when you died you went to heaven, as Duncan undoubtedly did, or to hell. People feared eternal damnation. Macbeth knows now that this is his fate.

Yet he still acts rashly, deciding to put on his armour and fight until the last: ***At least we'll die with harness on our back.*** Part of this is his training as a soldier, but mostly he is motivated by his arrogance and his tyrannical instincts. There is also the distinct possibility that he just does not care anymore: ***I 'gin to be aweary of the sun / And wish the estate o' the world were now undone.***

KEY **POINTS**

- *Lady Macbeth is dead. Her husband is scarcely moved by this news: she should have died hereafter.*

- *When the woods begin to move, Macbeth realises that he is not invincible.*

- *Macbeth lacks the intellect to think strategically. The only thing he seems capable of doing is lashing out with violence.*

ACT 5 SCENE VI

DUNSINANE. BEFORE THE CASTLE

Enter Malcolm, old Siward, Macduff, and their Army, with boughs. Drum and colours

Malcolm   Now near enough; your leavy[61] screens throw down,
And show like those you are. You, worthy uncle,
Shall with my cousin, your right noble son,
Lead our first battle. Worthy Macduff and we
Shall take upon 's what else remains to do,
According to our order.   5

Siward   Fare you well.
Do we but find the tyrant's power tonight,
Let us be beaten if we cannot fight.

Macduff   Make all our trumpets speak, give them all breath,
Those clamorous harbingers[62] of blood and death.   10

Exit

ANOTHER PART OF THE FIELD

Enter Macbeth

Macbeth Why should I play the Roman fool and die
On mine own sword?[69] While I see lives, the gashes
Do better upon them.

Enter Macduff

Macduff Turn, hell hound, turn!

Macbeth Of all men else I have avoided thee.   5
But get thee back, my soul is too much charg'd
With blood of thine already.

Macduff I have no words.
My voice is in my sword, thou bloodier villain
Than terms can give thee out!   10

They fight

Macbeth Thou losest labour.
As easy mayst thou the entrenchant air
With thy keen sword impress as make me bleed.[70]
Let fall thy blade on vulnerable crests;[71]
I bear a charmed life, which must not yield   15
To one of woman born.

Macduff Despair thy charm,
And let the angel whom thou still hast serv'd
Tell thee, Macduff was from his mother's womb
Untimely ripp'd.[72]   20

Macbeth Accursed be that tongue that tells me so,
For it hath cow'd my better part of man!
And be these juggling[73] fiends no more believ'd
That palter[74] with us in a double sense,
That keep the word of promise to our ear   25

[69] Roman soldiers would commit suicide rather than be captured by the enemy

This is a key quotation, as it shows that despite everything Macbeth does have a conscience of a sort

[70] Macbeth says Macduff could cut the air more easily than he could kill him, i.e. that it is impossible

[71] Heads

[72] Macduff was prematurely cut from his mother's womb, so wasn't 'born' in the normal sense

[73] Deceitful
[74] Trick

MACBETH

187

And break it to our hope. I'll not fight with thee.

Macduff
Then yield thee, coward,
And live to be the show and gaze o' the time.
We'll have thee, as our rarer monsters are,
Painted upon a pole, and underwrit,[75]   30
'Here may you see the tyrant.'

Macbeth
I will not yield,
To kiss the ground before young Malcolm's feet,
And to be baited with the rabble's curse.[76]
Though Birnam Wood be come to Dunsinane,   35
And thou oppos'd, being of no woman born,
Yet I will try the last. Before my body
I throw my warlike shield! Lay on, Macduff,
And damn'd be him that first cries, 'Hold, enough!'[77]

Exit fighting. Alarums

[75] *Written underneath*

[76] *The jeering of the crowds*

[77] *He hopes that the first to surrender will be damned*

KEY WORDS TO DESCRIBE HIM

ambitious
aspiring
zealous
purposeful
greedy
grasping
remorseful
wicked
regretful
insatiable
evil
malevolent
tyrannical
oppressor
inhuman
covetous
weak
ineffectual

MACBETH

199

to understand that he cannot have everything he wants. He thinks that to be a king all you have to do is wear a crown. The repetition of the clothing imagery supports this view. In many ways, Macbeth is a spoiled little boy playing dress-up. Not only can he never be the king that Duncan was, he does not have the slightest conception of what it takes to fill that role. The very first trait a king must demonstrate is complete and utter loyalty to his country. Macbeth never considers what his actions might actually do to Scotland. By killing Duncan and seizing the throne, Macbeth very nearly destroys his own country.

Macbeth is better suited to the battlefield than to kingship. He lacks the intellectual skills necessary to rule without being a tyrant. He responds violently to every problem. Macbeth knows that what he is doing is wrong but is unable to stop himself. He does not know how to exercise self-control, and his wife's stronger personality easily sways him.

Before he kills Duncan, Macbeth is beset by guilt, and had he been alone he would probably have abandoned his plan. It is Lady Macbeth's conviction that persuades him to murder Duncan. After the murder, however, Lady Macbeth realises that the husband she loved (the innocent Macbeth) is gone for ever. Faced with his moral disintegration and her own increasing guilt, she fades into the background as a character

and as a wife, leaving Macbeth more and more alone, and growing ever further apart from the highly regarded thane, admired warrior and beloved husband that we first meet.

In the aftermath of Duncan's murder, Macbeth, though in a state of shock, comprehends the horror of what he has done: *Will all great Neptune's ocean wash this blood / Clean from my hand? No, this my hand will rather / The multitudinous seas incarnadine, / Making the green one red.* Macbeth suppresses these feelings because his guilt is simply too much to bear. And by the time Duncan's murder is discovered, he is able to switch off any sense of guilt, and goes on to murder the two Grooms, then orders the deaths of Banquo, Lady Macduff and her children. Macbeth's moment of guilt ends all too quickly, and his killing continues right to the end of the play with the slaying of young Siward, not to mention the terrible things being done in his name throughout Scotland.

If Macbeth is to stop this murderous spree at any point, he must acknowledge that what he has done is wrong, but he is unable to do this because in his mind there is no turning back: *I am in blood / Stepp'd in so far that, should I wade no more, / Returning were as tedious as go o'er.* Yet Banquo's Ghost still haunts him despite his seeming indifference to ordering his friend's death. And he cannot, at first, bring himself to kill Macduff, after having slaughtered his family. This shows that Macbeth is not a psychopath. He does have a conscience, but he is too weak to resist his baser instincts.

As the play heads towards its tragic conclusion, Macbeth seems almost relieved. He thinks of all he has sacrificed in his blind quest for power:

> *I have liv'd long enough. My way of life*
> *Is fall'n into the sear, the yellow leaf,*
> *And that which should accompany old age,*
> *As honour, love, obedience, troops of friends,*
> *I must not look to have; but in their stead,*
> *Curses, not loud but deep, mouth-honour, breath,*
> *Which the poor heart would fain deny and dare not.*

His wife is dead, his guilt is universally known, and he has no friends and commands no respect. There could not be a character more opposite to the exemplary Duncan at this point.

By the final act, Macbeth seems ready to accept his fate. Surrounded by Macduff, Malcolm and the English army, Macbeth can return to the simpler life of a soldier. He is defiant as his enemies surround him: *At least we'll die with harness on our back.* One reason for this is his faith in the Witches' prophecies, but perhaps another more compelling reason is that he is doing what he knows best, fighting as a soldier. This reminds us that had he been happy with his already privileged life, none of this tragedy need have occurred. Macbeth hungered to be king, to wear a golden crown, but it is never clear to us why he wanted this so badly. Being king never gives him a moment's happiness. Perhaps what is truly depressing about Macbeth is that he learns absolutely nothing, and the redemption that the audience waits for never comes.

Macbeth fights at the beginning and at the end of this tragedy. The battles are polar opposites in what they represent. At the start he fights for the greater good, for his king and his God. At the end he is fighting to preserve his own corruption and attempting to defend what cannot be defended. His comparing himself to a bear being baited is apt: *They have tied me to a stake; I cannot fly, / But, bear-like, I must fight the course.* Macbeth's ignominious death and decapitation is a horrible perversion of the brave warrior so esteemed of the king. His legacy is to be named a 'dead butcher'. However, we must note his initial refusal to kill Macduff. Shakespeare's brilliant characterisation means that, right to the last, Macbeth remains a complex, fascinating character. What is most tragic is that he was capable of greatness, but utterly failed to achieve it.

L ADY MACBETH is a very interesting character, perhaps even more so than Macbeth. Her first act in the play is to read aloud Macbeth's letter and immediately resolve to kill Duncan: *The raven himself is hoarse / That croaks the fatal entrance of Duncan / Under my battlements.* She seems stronger and more determined than her husband at first. That a woman could be so ruthless must have been utterly shocking to Shakespeare's audience. Lady Macbeth, in fact, goes so far as to wish that she were not a woman at all so that she could murder Duncan herself. She knows that she will have to push Macbeth into doing so.

> *Hie thee hither,*
> *That I may pour my spirits in thine ear,*
> *And chastise with the valour of my tongue*
> *All that impedes thee from the golden round.*

She seems to see her sex as a handicap and asks the dark spirits to 'unsex' her, which hardly seems necessary to the audience, to whom she appears cold and ruthless already.

Come, you spirits / That tend on mortal thoughts, unsex me here … / Come to my woman's breasts, / And take my milk for gall.

Lady Macbeth manipulates her husband with ease. As his wife, she knows exactly how to do so. When he hesitates in killing Duncan, she repeatedly questions his manliness until he feels that the murder is no longer a choice but a necessity:

> *What beast was't, then,*
> *That made you break this enterprise to me?*
> *When you durst do it, then you were a man,*
> *And, to be more than what you were, you would*
> *Be so much more the man.*

But Lady Macbeth cannot actually kill Duncan herself (whether she intended to or not), and she has nothing to do with the murder of Banquo or any subsequent murders. Nor does she once express a desire to be queen. We can thus assume that this was not her primary motivation for plotting against Duncan, and that what she did, however terrible, was

ferocious

ambitious

androgynous

non-maternal

aspiring

zealous

purposeful
resolute

guilty

remorseful

regretful

penitent

redeemed

THERE IS A SAMPLE ESSAY ON
LADY MACBETH ON PAGE 235

out of love for Macbeth. Being king was obviously something he obsessed over. She wants him to be fulfilled and sees this as the only way he will be so. Her language is too dramatic and deliberately evil to be sincere. She plays the part of a woman who can involve herself in a murder without feeling guilty for it, but deep inside she is not really that woman.

Lady Macbeth may seem stronger than her husband at the start of the play, and she is certainly the dominant one in the relationship at that point, but their roles reverse completely. By the final act, Lady Macbeth is a truly pathetic sight, sleepwalking through the castle and trying desperately to wash off a bloodstain that will never go away. She cannot cope with the extent of her guilt. It is all-consuming and relentless. The fact that she apparently commits suicide shows that she cannot live with herself. Her conscience, however, also redeems her in the eyes of the audience and shows that first impressions can, in fact, be very wrong.

MACBETH

THE THREE WITCHES

THROUGHOUT THE play, the three Witches are used as visual spectacles as well as ominous portents of doom. They are tangible symbols of the evil that pervades this entire play. The Witches are hideous to look at, skinny and bearded, and they chant in rhyming couplets, which adds an extra acoustic element to the performance.

We first meet the Witches in the opening scene, when they let us know that *Fair is foul, and foul is fair,* meaning that the natural, or desirable, form of things has been altered. This is a very frightening idea. If good is evil and evil is good, then they cancel each other out, creating a moral vacuum where evil will thrive.

The three *black and midnight hags* plot mischief against Macbeth using charms, spells and prophecies. Their predictions prompt him to murder Duncan, to order the deaths of Banquo and his son, and to blindly believe in his own immortality. But do the Witches cause Macbeth's evil deeds or are they merely visible manifestations of the evil that already resides in his soul?

The Witches appear four times in the play: in Act I, Scene I; Act I, Scene III; Act III, Scene V and Act IV, Scene I.

Apart from the fact that they are servants of Hecate, we know little about the Witches' place in the world. In some ways they resemble the three Fates of Greek mythology, who dabbled in human affairs and caused much anguish. They clearly take a perverse delight in using their knowledge of the future to toy with and destroy human beings. Yet, as Macbeth has free will, it is he, and not the Witches, who must bear the ultimate responsibility for his own evil acts.

Dramatically, the Witches add much to the play. Their scenes are exciting and entertaining in a very dark way. Act IV, Scene I is the highpoint of the play for many audiences and arguably one of the most iconic dramatic moments of all time.

KEY WORDS TO DESCRIBE THEM

weird

evil

mischievous

bizarre

malevolent

dangerous

powerful

wicked

gross

manipulative

clairvoyant

*THERE IS A SAMPLE ESSAY ON
THE WITCHES ON PAGE 226*

BANQUO

B ANQUO IS an enigmatic and intriguing character. Like Macbeth, we hear about Banquo before we meet him – *they doubly redoubled strokes upon the foe* – and it is clear that he is just as brave and fearless as Macbeth. Duncan often pairs the two as equals: *They smack of honour both.* Yet it is Macbeth who is awarded the disgraced Thane of Cawdor's lands and titles. This tells us that he is of a higher social rank than Banquo.

In Shakespeare's day, no relationship was considered quite as important as the friendship between men. Many of Shakespeare's sonnets celebrate male platonic camaraderie. The fact that these two men fought together is more significant still, for to fight alongside a friend was to create an indissoluble bond.

It is significant that the Witches are waiting for Macbeth, not Banquo. In fact, they ignore him until he initiates communication: *Speak then to me, who neither beg nor fear / Your favours nor your hate.* The Witches slyly address him as *Lesser than Macbeth, and greater;* and *Not so happy, yet much happier.* Like much of what the Witches say, this is equivocation. Banquo is lesser in the sense that he is not of as high a social rank as Macbeth, but greater because of how cynical, sceptical and circumspect he is. He is also perceptive: *why do you start and seem to fear / Things that do sound so fair?*

Banquo's role is as a foil to Macbeth; that is his primary dramatic function. He tries to warn Macbeth to use caution: *oftentimes to win us to our harm, / The instruments of darkness tell us truths / Win us with honest trifles, to betray 's / In deepest consequence.* Banquo sees that the Witches may actually be using their prior knowledge of the awarding of the Thanedom of Cawdor to incite Macbeth to do something rash. This shows both intelligence and loyalty. Banquo seems quite indifferent to the Witches; he neither implores nor fears *Your favours nor your hate.* And yet the Witches' prophecy – *Thou shalt get kings, though thou be none* – makes an impact on him. A more gradual impact than on Macbeth, but an impact nonetheless.

KEY WORDS TO DESCRIBE HIM

cautious
loyal
wise
noble
moral
ambitious
brave
honest
sensible
conflicted
steadfast
strong
logical

MACBETH
207

Like Macbeth, Banquo has a reputation as an honourable man. We hear it in Duncan's lavish praise: ***True, worthy Banquo! He is full so valiant / … a peerless kinsman.*** And certainly, until Act II, there is nothing to suggest the Witches' words have had the type of effect on Banquo's character that they had on Macbeth's. In Act II, however, Shakespeare reveals another side to Banquo, using one of his favourite symbols to suggest immoral thoughts or actions – an inability to sleep: ***A heavy summons lies like lead upon me / And yet I would not sleep.*** And when he does finally sleep, we learn that Banquo has disturbing thoughts: ***Merciful powers, / Restrain in me the cursed thoughts that nature / Gives way to in repose!***

But is it really surprising that Banquo is obviously preoccupied with the Witches' prophecy? Is it not natural for a father to be ambitious for his children, and his children's children? The key point is that, unlike Macbeth, Banquo's thoughts do not manifest themselves in murder. Even so, we must ask the question, would this have happened in time? The Witches' prediction, after all, did not provoke a dramatic or immediate reaction in him, but an insidious one.

Banquo is the last person Macbeth speaks to (except for a servant) before the murder of Duncan. He confides to Macbeth: ***I dreamt last night of the three weird sisters: / To you they have show'd some truth.*** There is nothing to suggest here that Banquo has any inkling of what Macbeth is planning. He is clear about the fact that he only wants to discuss the Witches and that he is still loyal to Duncan: ***but still keep / My bosom franchis'd and allegiance clear, / I shall be counsell'd.***

Following Macduff's discovery of Duncan's body, Banquo is given little dialogue, so it is up to the actor playing him to express his reaction physically – with meaningful glances, for example. The few lines Banquo does say seem sincere: ***Too cruel anywhere. / Dear Duff, I prithee, contradict thyself, / And say it is not so.*** Banquo may be distraught, but his silence certainly contrasts with Macduff's eloquent articulation of his grief, not to mention Macbeth's melodramatic and empty words.

In Act III, Scene I, Banquo definitely knows the truth: ***Thou hast it now: King, Cawdor, Glamis, all, / As the weird women promised, and I fear / Thou play'dst most foully for't.*** But still he stays silent. His crime seems a small one compared to Macbeth's, but silence can allow evil to flourish, and that is definitely the case here. Instead of publicly accusing Macbeth, however, Banquo is eager to stay on his

BANQUO

side. He promises to attend Macbeth's banquet, whereas Macduff quite deliberately snubs the occasion. Banquo even wonders if he can hope for great things, too: *May they not be my oracles as well / And set me up in hope?* This is a serious moral lapse on Banquo's part, even if it is done out of love for his son, Fleance.

Banquo's final conversation with Macbeth is darkly funny, in a way, when Banquo tells Macbeth his exact itinerary. It obviously does not occur to him that he is in danger, despite the fact that Macbeth is capable of murder. And, here, in his first act as king, Macbeth displays just how murderous he is when he hires assassins to kill his best friend and comrade in arms.

Banquo's role in the play does not end with his death; his Ghost haunts Macbeth. The Ghost is a guilty hallucination on Macbeth's part, but it alerts the assembled nobility to the fact that something is terribly wrong in Scotland.

Banquo's final appearance in the play is in Act IV, Scene I, when Macbeth is horrified to see him lead a trail of kings in the fourth Apparition, showing that the Witches' prophecy will eventually come true.

Thou hast it now: King, Cawdor, Glamis, all,
As the weird women promised, and I fear
Thou play'dst most foully for't

– BANQUO (ACT III SCENE I)

DUNCAN

DUNCAN IS the perfect king: *Duncan / Hath borne his faculties so meek, hath been / So clear in his great office.* But the fact that Duncan is such a good king is also incidental. He is the rightful king by blood ties alone. Ironically, Macbeth is the one who praises Duncan the most, and talks about what a great king he is, before deciding to kill him.

Duncan is an exemplary, guiltless, innocent character. His primary role is to serve as a complete contrast to Macbeth.

It is important to remember that Duncan's innocence would not have been seen in a negative light. On the contrary, innocence was a highly esteemed characteristic in Shakespeare's day. We might think that Duncan's misplaced trust in Cawdor shows poor judgment, but Shakespeare's audience may well have thought that Duncan, being such a good man himself, was simply incapable of seeing the bad in others. Similarly, Duncan wishes to reward Macbeth for the service he has given Scotland on the battlefield: *I have begun to plant thee, and will labour / To make thee full of growing.* These generous words seem highly ironic to us in the light of what follows, but the incident highlights Duncan's pure spirit. Having said that, there is no doubt that Duncan is also firm and is certainly not afraid to dole out punishment when it is necessary. He orders Cawdor to be executed, for example: *Is execution done on Cawdor?* Duncan possesses all the traits necessary to be a truly good king; he is kind, temperate, just, trusting and trustworthy, yet also firm and brave. His murder really is a tragedy.

KEY WORDS TO DESCRIBE HIM

benevolent
valiant
divinely appointed
beloved
kind
wise

trusting

virtuous
gracious
harmless
kingly
brave
firm
noble
dutiful

THERE IS A SAMPLE ESSAY ON
KINGSHIP ON PAGE 230

MACBETH

211

MACDUFF

THE CHARACTER of Macduff acts as an adversary to Macbeth. He is also a thane and is obviously close to Duncan. Aside from Banquo, Macduff is the first person to suspect Macbeth; we know this from the way he heads straight to London and misses Macbeth's coronation in Scone. This was a deliberate insult to Macbeth. The murder of Macduff's family that follows serves two main purposes:

- It shows the depths of evil to which Macbeth has sunk. His attack on Macduff's family is an attack on the smallest unit of society.
- It provides Macduff with a personal reason to pursue Macbeth and thus lends a sense of poetic justice to the resolution of the play.

Some feel that having two adversaries to Macbeth – Macduff and Malcolm – lessens the impact of both characters. However, Macduff's role is a major one, and Shakespeare gives him some great lines, particularly in the aftermath of his family being killed:

I must also feel it as a man:
I cannot but remember such things were
That were most precious to me. Did Heaven look on,
And would not take their part? Sinful Macduff,
They were all struck for thee! Naught that I am,
Not for their own demerits, but for mine,
Fell slaughter on their souls.

Macduff's loyalty to Scotland is evident in the sacrifice he makes to restore the rightful heir to the throne. He pays an enormous price for his loyalty, one that a modern audience might question.

This terrible tragedy makes Macduff the perfect candidate to end Macbeth's reign of terror. Macduff gets to avenge his wife and children in the final scene of the play. He cannot articulate his grief but lets his sword speak for him: *I have no words. / My voice is in my sword, thou bloodier villain / Than terms can give thee out!*

KEY WORDS TO DESCRIBE HIM

sharp
loyal
calm

purposeful

responsible
grief-stricken
brave
honest
resourceful
triumphant
strong
courageous
sensitive

MACBETH

213

MALCOLM

MALCOLM GROWS up during the course of the drama. The scared prince of the first act grows into a fitting replacement for great Duncan by the end of the play. We know he is young because he is innocent and has never known a woman. But he is forced to grow up quickly, first when his father dies, and then when he has to lead an army to win back his country.

Malcolm's potential to be a great king is clearly seen in Act 4, Scene IV. Malcolm uses good judgment when he tests Macduff's loyalty instead of automatically trusting him. Malcolm satisfies himself that he is not dealing with another Macbeth, and this is commendable. He also speaks eloquently, in a way that is reminiscent of Duncan's gracious speech in his choice of words and emphasis.

Macduff, this noble passion,
Child of integrity, hath from my soul
Wip'd the black scruples, reconcil'd my thoughts
To thy good truth and honour. Devilish Macbeth
By many of these trains hath sought to win me
Into his power, and modest wisdom plucks me
From over-credulous haste

Throughout Act V, Malcolm's leadership is admirable. He is very much his father's son. Scotland needs Malcolm on the throne, not just because Macbeth is a tyrant, but also because Malcolm is the rightful heir. Malcolm will clearly be a great king, and all the stronger for what he has endured.

Shakespeare's audience believed in hereditary monarchy. They would have happily cheered Malcolm's ascension to the throne.

weak

scared

inexperienced

intelligent

virginal

shrewd

fair

patient

courageous

cunning

resourceful

wise

calm

kingly

gracious

IMPORTANT
THEMES
IN MACBETH

AMBITION

Ambition was considered a dangerous thing in Shakespeare's day, and sometimes people were hanged merely on suspicion of being too ambitious. Thus, in *Macbeth* we find a powerful exploration of ambition and how corrupting it is when it goes unchecked by any sort of moral constraints. The same applies to other emotions that are not held in some kind of moral check. Any human emotion can be destructive if taken to excess.

We see the effect of ambition on three characters: Macbeth, Lady Macbeth and Banquo. We see how these different individuals respond to the same innate characteristic.

Macbeth's ambition is the catalyst for the entire play, though we never learn why he wants to be king as much as he does: ***I have no spur / To prick the sides of my intent, but only / Vaulting ambition.*** He does not seem to have any aptitude for the job! But perhaps that is the real point that Shakespeare is making, that sometimes an individual just wants something to the extent that their whole identity rests upon it, and they will do anything at all to achieve it.

Lady Macbeth is ambitious for her husband. Ambition on behalf of someone else, particularly a family member, is seen as more acceptable. In many ways, however, it can be even more destructive. Macbeth was willing to walk away from his ambition, but Lady Macbeth forced him into committing an evil deed which then snowballed into chaos: ***When you durst do it, then you were a man.*** A modern – albeit not murderous – equivalent might be seen in the activities of a 'showbiz mom' whose ambition for her child may be overwhelming.

Banquo is slow to react to ambition, but by Act III it is definitely creeping up on him: *May they not be my oracles as well, / And set me up in hope?* However, it is important to note that Banquo's ambition is for his son, Fleance, and not for himself. As well as that, Malcolm and Macduff are ambitious to restore Scotland to its former glory. So ambition is only bad when it is selfish and immoral.

GOOD VERSUS EVIL

Most Shakespearean tragedies set good and evil in opposition, and Macbeth is no different in this regard. However, while there is the usual external battling of good versus evil (Duncan, Macduff and Malcolm versus Macbeth and Lady Macbeth), what makes this play so interesting is that we also have an internal battle between good and evil within the characters themselves.

Macbeth tries to suppress his evil side several times, but in vain: *I see thee still, / And on thy blade and dudgeon gouts of blood, / Which was not so before.* Macbeth wants to be good but lacks the self-belief to resist his wife's manipulation. And once he has committed his first murder, he lacks the self-discipline to stop. *To be thus is nothing / But to be safely thus.*

Lady Macbeth, on the other hand, tries to suppress her good side, but this, too, is in vain. She shows signs of scruples from the very start, when she has to bolster her courage with drink, but she makes a fatal mistake in ignoring her conscience and pays dearly for it. *Out, damned spot!*

The theme of good versus evil is a universal and timeless one, and as long as humans live on the earth, the two will be in fierce conflict.

Duncan, Macduff and Malcolm uphold good and virtue, no matter what the personal cost may be. Macduff pays a heavy price for saving Scotland, but he feels no cost is too high to achieve goodness and justice.

KINGSHIP

In the play, Duncan is always referred to as a **king**, while Macbeth soon becomes known as the **tyrant**. A true king offers his kingdom order and justice, as well as comfort and affection. Under him, subjects are rewarded according to their merits, as when Duncan makes Macbeth Thane of Cawdor to reward his performance in the war against Norway.

Most important, the king must put loyalty to Scotland above his own interests. Macbeth, by contrast, puts his own interests first. He brings chaos to Scotland, as symbolised by the bad weather and bizarre supernatural events that unfold, and he offers no real justice, only a habit of wilfully murdering those he sees as a threat to his authority. The very fact that Macbeth murders Duncan in the first place tells us that he will always put his own ambitions before Scotland.

Macbeth only sees the **golden round**, the outward trappings of being king. He lacks the intellect even to conceive of all that is involved in being king.

THERE IS A SAMPLE ESSAY ON THE THEME OF KINGSHIP ON PAGE 230

HOW TO WRITE ESSAYS
ON MACBETH

In the Leaving Certificate exam, you will always have the choice of two essays on *Macbeth*. The essay is worth 60 marks, which is 15 per cent of your total marks for English.

Your essay should consist of: an introduction (which repeats the wording of the question), approximately six paragraphs (although you can write more) which deal with one point or one topic each, and a conclusion (which refers back to the question and ties up any loose ends).

Throughout your essay, you must answer the question. Only deal with what is asked; stay focused, and do not waffle or go off the point! Remember, you only get marks for relevant points. You must also quote as much as possible, and you should also refer to the text. Two quotations per paragraph would be ideal, but it is quality, not quantity, which counts. Remember, you can pick quotations that are versatile and can be used in lots of different essays. For example, when Malcolm says, ***The night is long which never finds the day***… you could use this quotation for a question on Macduff or Malcolm or kingship.

There are four possible styles of question for any Shakespearean text.

1. On a theme (see sample essay on kingship on page 230)
2. On a character
3. On imagery or style or on a specific scene (see sample essay on imagery on page 232)
4. An opinion question; for example, 'Is *Macbeth* still relevant to a modern audience?'

The character who comes up most often in a question on his

own is Macbeth. Next is Lady Macbeth. Less often there is a question on a character such as Banquo or Macduff. Sometimes there is a question on the Witches. Any of the main themes can come up. A stylistic question on imagery, which occurs from time to time, may seem quite difficult, but the main thing is to know relevant quotations.

When answering a question on *Macbeth:*

• Always write about the play chronologically – go from the very first scene onwards.

• Start by underlining the important words in the question to make sure you know exactly what the examiner is looking for. In your answer, keep repeating the wording of the question to demonstrate clear focus.

• Do not summarise the play. The examiner will assume you have a thorough knowledge of it and is looking for your ability to analyse, not summarise.

• If the question takes the form of a statement with which you are asked to agree or disagree, as a general rule it is better to agree. Of course there are exceptions, but mostly it is easier to argue for the statement than against it.

• Shape the question to your individual needs. Make it work for you. For example, if you are asked about the scene you considered most dramatic and you know all about the Witches, then pick Act IV, Scene I. Or if you are asked what makes the play enjoyable and you know Lady Macbeth's character well, say that you enjoyed Shakespeare's

characterisation, particularly Lady Macbeth.

• Plan your answer carefully. A plan should consist of six to ten points that you can develop throughout the essay. This will ensure that you do not:

1. run out of ideas after a page or two
2. become irrelevant
3. spend too much time exploring just one or two issues, or spend too much time on just one character
4. run out of time
5. forget any quotations that pop into your mind. You can simply jot them on your plan and slip them in where appropriate.

When you are preparing for your Leaving Certificate, have pen and paper in hand and plan, plan, plan! Whether it is a bubble plan, a spider plan or bullet points, once you get used to planning, it is easy to do well in this question.

Lastly:

• Use personal opinion. 'I' is the most important word in any Leaving Certificate English essay!

• Refer to a performance (either a play or a film) you have seen. Remember, this is a drama.

• Refer to the original audience, for whom, let's not forget, Shakespeare wrote this play.

SAMPLE PLANS
ON MACBETH

Below are examples of some of the most common questions on *Macbeth* and advice on how to tackle the essay titles. Before you start any essay, however, forget about having the text open in front of you as you write. Learn off your quotations, read through your notes, then shut your books and do the question in 50 to 60 minutes. This may sound tough, but you must recreate exam conditions as closely as possible in order to get the best possible mark.

SAMPLE PLAN 1

'We feel very little pity for the central characters of Macbeth and Lady Macbeth in Shakespeare's play.'
To what extent would you agree with the above view? Support your answer by reference to the play.

Introduction: I will start by saying I both agree and disagree with the statement. I agree that we tend to feel very little pity for Macbeth, but I disagree regarding Lady Macbeth. I think most people do tend to pity her.

Paragraph 1: Macbeth's jealousy of Duncan seems completely unfair given the latter's kindness to him.

Paragraph 2: Macbeth makes the decision to embrace the dark side. Yes, he was pushed by his wife, but this does not excuse him.

Paragraph 3: Macbeth keeps killing and never really sees the error of his ways. He fights to the bitter end and dies an utterly shameful and pitiless death. Yet, we have some pity for him when he cannot fight Macduff.

Paragraph 4: Though Lady Macbeth pushes her husband into murder, she does this out of love for him. She is a loyal, if misguided, wife. Also, she is unable to murder Duncan herself and has to drink to give herself courage.

Paragraph 5: She is innocent of all subsequent murders. Macbeth seems to know that she would not approve. She starts to fall apart from the moment she faints in Act II.

Paragraph 6: Act V, Scene I ensures we feel great pity for Lady Macbeth. She has been destroyed by what she has done. Her suicide emphasises this total repentance on her part.

Once you have your plan done, it is easy to form your introduction and your conclusion.

Sample introduction: I agree that we tend to feel very little pity for Macbeth. Although Macbeth begins as a hero and certainly has real difficulty in overcoming his scruples regarding the murder of Duncan, the comparative ease with which he has Banquo and Macduff's family killed negates any sympathy which we might otherwise have felt for him. Regarding his enigmatic wife, I disagree with the statement that we feel very little pity for her. I think most people do tend to pity her. She may first appear to deserve the title of 'fiend-like queen', but her utter disintegration in Act V, Scene 1 shows us otherwise. The cold-hearted manipulator of Act I and Act II is, in my view, a consummate actress trying to do what she thinks is best for her ambitious husband. In this essay I will discuss Macbeth and Lady Macbeth

separately in order to prove the central premise of my argument.

Sample conclusion: In conclusion, I agree that we feel little pity for the character of Macbeth. After all, a man who murders a fine old king for his own selfish ends, then his best friend and finally an innocent woman and her children is hardly worthy of our compassion. However, a woman who does a terrible thing, but out of love for her husband, and who cannot live with the guilt and subsequently kills herself naturally arouses our sympathy. Before forgiveness and pity, there must be remorse. Macbeth's remorse is simply too little, too late. His wife, however, literally cannot live with herself, and her regret and horror at what she has done is compelling. Both characters are wonderful examples of Shakespeare's magnificent characterisation. Macbeth's downward spiral into an evil he cannot return from is all too realistic, while Lady Macbeth's crippled conscience gives us hope that good will always win out in the end.

SAMPLE PLAN 2

*'In **Macbeth**, Shakespeare presents us with a powerful vision of evil.'*
Write your response to the above statement. Textual support may include reference to a particular performance of the play you have seen.

Introduction: Agree with the statement: '*Macbeth* is indeed a powerful exploration of evil, and the far-reaching repercussions of any evil act.' Refer to any production of *Macbeth* that you might have seen (including film).

Paragraph 1: Duncan is completely innocent, and his death signals the death of good and the birth of evil.

Paragraph 2: We see that evil is not abstract, but a potential reality in the way Macbeth actively chooses the evil path. This too is powerful.

Paragraph 3: Lady Macbeth's role in the murder shows that sometimes people commit evil deeds out of good motives (love for her husband), and this too is disturbing because we like to think that 'evil' people are a separate species.

Paragraph 4: Banquo's silence is also evil for it enables Macbeth to carry out the subsequent murders. Banquo's silence leads to his own downfall.

Paragraph 5: The murder of Macduff's family also presents a powerful vision of evil. Most of us believe that even criminals would not hurt a child. What could be more evil than killing an innocent mother and her children?

Paragraph 6: Discuss the nature of evil and how you personally would define evil. Also, discuss the ending of the play and how Macbeth cannot bring himself to kill Macduff. Does good win out within Macbeth's soul as well as in the play as a whole? How did seeing *Macbeth* performed affect your understanding of this theme?

Sample conclusion: In conclusion, I certainly agree that

in *Macbeth* Shakespeare presents us with a powerful vision of evil. It is hard for us to reconcile ourselves to the idea that evil dwells among us, not just in the heart of a cruel dictator in a far-off country, but in those around us. Shakespeare explores evil in a discomfiting way. He shows that people do not have to be born evil to commit evil acts. He shows us that evil does not merely reside in those who have had terrible childhoods and deprived lives. He shows us that evil is a choice, one we all face, and he shows that to let bad emotion get the better of us, whether it is ambition, jealousy or hatred, will ultimately destroy us. *Macbeth* is a lesson in self-discipline as much as anything else, and Shakespeare teaches us that there are no shortcuts in life – you must work honestly to really achieve anything. I personally feel that, at this moment in history, *Macbeth* is more relevant than ever. It is only when we confront the darkness in our world by staring it in the face that we will conquer it.

SAMPLE PLAN 3

'In Shakespeare's Macbeth *the evil characters are presented in a far more interesting way than the good characters.'*
To what extent would you agree with the above view? Support your answer by reference to the play.

Introduction: I agree that in *Macbeth* the evil characters tend to be characterised in a more interesting way than the good characters, although there are exceptions (Banquo). I do agree that Macbeth, Lady Macbeth and the

the presence of witches in their society. His contemporary audience would have been terrified by the onstage presence of the Witches, and Shakespeare plays upon this fear to create terror and suspense.

Horror and science fiction are still thriving genres. Indeed the title song of one of the Harry Potter blockbusters is taken from *Macbeth* (Act IV, Scene I): 'By the pricking of my thumbs / Something wicked this way comes.' So, it seems to be part of the human psyche to have a kind of appalled fascination with creatures such as the 'black and midnight hags', and of course Shakespeare, with his extraordinary psychological insight, capitalised on this.

The first scene of any film or play is hugely significant, and Shakespeare always carefully crafted the opening moments of his plays. Therefore, the Witches' presence in Act I, Scene I sets the tone for the entire play. Their first words are later echoed by Macbeth himself: 'Fair is foul and foul is fair.' This means that good is bad and bad is good, and so neither means anything. A world without moral order is a scary, frightening thing. We, the audience, know the natural order of things has gone awry, and we wonder what is going to be played out in front of us.

At this point we do not know who the Witches are or what they want with Macbeth. But now his name has been mentioned, the audience is alert to other mentions of him, and these come in abundance in the next scene (Act I, Scene II) when we hear of a brave, fearless warrior, a champion of Scottish freedom, much beloved of his king. What, we wonder, could the Witches want with such a

man? The device of the three Witches is an appropriate beginning to this play.

Our next meeting with the Witches is in Act I, Scene III. At first the Witches are by themselves, discussing their evil deeds with obvious glee and delight. Even at this early stage, we can see that these creatures, whatever they are, are entirely without conscience or pity. Banquo immediately comments on the unsettling appearance of the Witches: 'What are these / So wither'd and so wild in their attire, / That look not like the inhabitants o' the earth … / You should be women, / And yet your beards forbid me to interpret / That you are so.' The Witches speak to Macbeth. They refer to him as the Thane of Glamis, which he is, but also as the Thane of Cawdor, and as 'King hereafter'. In the previous scene we learned the Duncan intended to make Macbeth Thane of Cawdor as a reward for his valour in battle. This dramatic irony creates suspense: how can the Witches know this?

Macbeth, for his part, physically jumps at their prophecy, and in contrast to the sceptical Banquo seems to put altogether too much store in the Witches' words. The Witches have the uncanny ability to say what the men want to hear. They tell Banquo, 'Thou shalt get kings, though thou be none,' and he is amused and pleased at the thought of his descendants becoming kings. Macbeth, however, clearly has an agenda. When Ross and Angus arrive to inform Macbeth he is to be Thane of Cawdor, and that the old thane is to be executed for treason, both men are amazed. Macbeth's ambition to have the rest of the prophecy come true is clear to us in his aside: 'Glamis, and Thane of Cawdor! / The greatest is behind.' Banquo sagely warns Macbeth: 'oftentimes, to win us to our harm, / The instruments of darkness tell us truths, / Win us with honest trifles, to betray 's / In deepest consequence.' Banquo quite rightly sees that the Witches are titillating Macbeth, and that, ultimately, they wish his downfall and not his triumph.

Macbeth is all too ready to believe that the next part of the prophecy will come true, indeed has to come true. It is very obvious that Macbeth has wanted to be king for a very long time. 'Two truths are told, / As happy prologues to the swelling act / Of the imperial theme.' It is disturbing to see how quickly Macbeth's thoughts turn to murder: 'My thought, whose murder yet is but fantastical …' Macbeth's inner turmoil is fascinating to the audience. The Witches were a catalyst to this already changed Macbeth, yet they do not force him into anything. They certainly do not mention murdering Duncan. They say he will be king, and perhaps, if he had been patient, that would have come to pass. On the other hand, the Witches may be visual manifestations of the evil that already lurks in Macbeth's heart. They do not so much plant the seed as water the one which was already there.

It is also important to note that Macbeth writes to his wife as an insurance against changing his mind, in my opinion. Both the Witches and Lady Macbeth are blamed for the murder of Duncan, but ultimately it is Macbeth who actually does the wicked deed. The Witches are vital at this point precisely because they make us question

Macbeth, and they muddy the waters of morality, which makes for interesting debate and conjecture.

The only consistent thing about the Witches is their inconsistency. They appear sporadically, and we do not know when to expect them, which adds to the suspense, exactly what Shakespeare intended. In Act III, Scene V, we meet Hecate, goddess of witchcraft and the only deity to appear in the play, which is significant. Many critics have claimed that Shakespeare didn't write this scene and that it was added at a later date by another writer. In any case, it certainly heightens the tension and also creates dramatic irony. Hecate berates the Witches for not involving her thus far. She is also critical of their choice of Macbeth, saying he is unworthy of their attentions: 'all you have done / Hath been but for a wayward son, / Spiteful and wrathful, who, as others do, / Loves for his own ends, not for you.' She promises to contribute to Macbeth's downfall, and as he has already committed regicide and had his best friend murdered, the audience is primed for the worst.

Towards the end of Act III, Macbeth resolves to seek out the Witches. So, instead of stumbling across evil as he did in Act I, Macbeth is actively seeking it out. This is an important distinction and serves to highlight the fact that Macbeth is very much a changed man. In Act IV, Scene I the Witches play out their last scene in the play, and it is as shocking, disturbing and as rich a visual spectacle as we could ask for, and absolutely essential to the play. The Witches always speak in rhyming couplets (the rest of the play is in blank verse). This gives the effect of a chant, a spell, which is of course deliberate. In this famous scene, the Witches concoct a hideous brew: 'Double, double, toil and trouble; / Fire burn and cauldron bubble.' The ingredients, even by our desensitised standards, are truly horrific: toad's sweat, a witch's corpse, the nose of a Turk, the finger of a baby born to a prostitute (and then strangled) in a ditch, the blood of a sow that has eaten her litter … One can only imagine the terror of Shakespeare's own audience, who truly believed in the actual presence of witches. In fact, an estimated nine million 'witches' were killed in the 16th, 17th and 18th centuries. This scene is the climax of the play. It demonstrates Macbeth's absolute descent into evil, and that is its dramatic purpose.

From this evil potion come four Apparitions. All of the Apparitions are cleverly devised and have resonances with later parts of the play. Collectively, they make Macbeth feel invincible, but also paranoid. Ultimately, they make him feel that he has nothing to lose, and this is when he becomes truly dangerous.

The first Apparition is an armed head (a head wearing a helmet, like Macbeth's own decapitated head at the end of the play). This head warns him to 'Beware Macduff, / Beware the Thane of Fife'. The second Apparition is a bloody child (perhaps Macduff's son), who predicts that 'none of woman born / Shall harm Macbeth'. This misleads Macbeth into thinking he is invincible, but the first Apparition has already made him fear Macduff. The third Apparition is a child carrying a branch who predicts that 'Macbeth shall never vanquish'd be until / Great Birnam Wood to high Dunsinane Hill / Shall come against him.' It is the final Apparition which disturbs Macbeth greatly. It is a succession of eight kings, who all resemble Banquo. The last king carries a glass. Macbeth is reminded of the original prophecy, but although he attempts to question the Witches as to the meaning of this, they disappear. Their work in the play is done. They have used their knowledge of the future to pervert and disturb the present. They, evil incarnate, are the only ones in the play to refer to Macbeth as a great king: 'Come, sisters, cheer we up his sprites, / And show the best of our delights. / I'll charm the air to give a sound, / While you perform your antic round, / That this great King may kindly say / Our duties did his welcome pay.'

In conclusion, as I have demonstrated throughout my essay, the Witches add much to *Macbeth*. From their first appearance, the Witches' presence alerts us to the fact that something is very wrong in Scotland. Though they only appear sporadically, it is this unpredictability which fascinates the audience. Their obvious glee in their evil actions is also central to the theme of 'Fair is foul and foul is fair'. The cauldron scene is unapologetically melodramatic, and Shakespeare allows his sinister creations space to wallow in their hateful acts. I cannot imagine Macbeth without the Witches, and that, I feel, is proof enough that they are absolutely essential to the plot.

SAMPLE ESSAY 2

Write an essay in which you explore the theme of kingship in Shakespeare's *Macbeth*. Support your answer with reference to the play.

I found the theme of kingship to be a fascinating one during my study of the riveting play *Macbeth*. Not only was it interesting to compare and contrast the kings' different styles of leadership, but I also found the whole concept of kingship intriguing. In Shakespeare's era, kings and queens were considered sacred beings. Not only had they a God-given right to rule, but they were also God's representatives on earth. Anyone who usurped the natural order of hereditary monarchy would cause chaos. We see this chaos when Macbeth kills Duncan – 'this sore night / Hath trifled former knowings' – as even nature revolts again Macbeth's unlawful reign. Kingship affects everyone. A good king will create a good society, but a bad one will cause evil. We also learned about Queen Elizabeth I and King James I, and I think Shakespeare makes some sly allusions to their reigns in this play, which makes it even more interesting!

The first king we meet is Duncan, who is undoubtedly a good man to the very core. He is referred to as a 'great King', 'gracious Duncan' and 'a most sainted King', so we know he is loved by his subjects. Not only is Duncan generous to those who have served him well – 'I have begun to plant thee, and will labour / To make thee full of growing' – but he is also firm with the likes of Cawdor, and

orders his men to 'Go pronounce his present death'. Duncan impresses us, the audience, with his exemplary chivalry, and ironically it is Macbeth himself who articulates Duncan's many qualities: 'this Duncan / Hath born his faculties so meek, hath been / So clear in his great office, that his virtues / Will plead like angels'. Duncan is a gentle man in every sense of the word.

If Duncan has a fault it is that he is too trusting, too ready to give others the benefit of the doubt. He judges people by his own high standards and admits, 'There's no art / To find the mind's construction in the face'. He had no suspicions about either Cawdor – 'He was a gentleman on whom I built / An absolute trust' – or Macbeth: 'O valiant cousin! Worthy gentleman!' But while a modern audience might consider this a flaw, I think Shakespeare's audience would have had a different view. Innocence was prized then, especially as it emulated Christ. Duncan really is a perfect king in my view, and so there is absolutely no justification for what Macbeth does. He commits a repulsive crime of betrayal when he kills Duncan. He knows this too, and acknowledges it when he says: 'He's here in double trust'.

After the murder of Duncan, once Malcolm and Donalbain have fled, Macbeth is crowned King of Scotland. Yet it is still unclear why he wants to be king. As he says nothing about policy or strategy, we may assume that it is power and 'the golden round' which he desires. In other words, Macbeth wants to be king for all the wrong reasons. The first characteristic a king must have is loyalty to his country above all. By killing Duncan, Macbeth shows ultimate disloyalty. By contrast, his fellow thane, Macduff, gives up everything for Scotland: 'in that rawness left you wife and child'. Because of his evil usurping, Macbeth can never use the kingship to achieve good. In fact, his Machiavellian scheming ensures just the opposite.

Macbeth's first act as king is to have his best friend, his comrade in battle, Banquo, killed: 'To be thus is nothing / But to be safely thus.' This time he hires assassins to do his dirty work. This murder, so personal, seemed somehow worse to me than the regicide of Duncan. Even Macbeth's first banquet is a disaster, for his guilt manifests itself in his belief that he sees Banquo's Ghost: 'Thou canst not say I did it; never shake / Thy gory locks at me.' Not only is Macbeth capable of terrible deeds, but he is also incapable of dealing with them.

In fact, the only characters who refer to Macbeth as a king are the Witches. The fact that he seeks them out in the horrific Act IV, Scene I is further proof of his sheer inability to rule, or even to stand on his own two feet. His decision to let the 'firstlings' of his heart be the 'firstlings' of his hands is also the opposite of how a king should react. A king should think hard, and be measured and careful in all he does. Macbeth never stops acting as a soldier, for that is his true profession. He lashes out and hurts all those around him. He almost destroys Scotland. 'It weeps, it bleeds, and each new day a gash / Is added to her wounds.'

By contrast, the potential of using the kingship to achieve good is truly seen in King Edward of England, Edward the Confessor. Edward is described in godlike terms: 'He hath a heavenly gift of prophecy, / And sundry blessings hang about his throne / That speak him full of grace.' Edward can predict the future and heal the sick. He also gives Malcolm safe refuge, even though he is endangering England's relations with Scotland by doing so. Edward is practical, too. He sends his own men to restore Malcolm, and thus order, to the throne. In short, Edward is a perfect king. He is a rebuke to Macbeth. In comparison with him, Macbeth is merely a tyrant.

Malcolm is the rightful heir to the Scottish throne. He is Duncan's son and the Prince of Cumberland. Therefore, God has chosen him. Although Malcolm is young and inexperienced, his instincts are always good. This was clear to me when Malcolm wisely fled from Scotland in the aftermath of his father's murder. 'This murderous shaft that's shot / Hath not yet lighted'. But we really get to know Malcolm in Act IV, Scene III when he tests Macduff in a rather roundabout and childish way by pretending he is worse than Macbeth! 'There's no bottom, none, / In my voluptuousness.' This shows that Malcolm is his father's son – with the added benefit of not trusting indiscriminately. Also, Malcolm knows exactly what it takes to be a king: 'The king-becoming graces / As justice, verity, temperance, stableness, / Bounty, perseverance, mercy, lowliness, / Devotion, patience, courage, fortitude.' And even at such a tender age, we see how he comforts Macduff: 'The night is long that never finds the day.' Clearly, Malcolm should be king.

The clothing imagery in Macbeth is used, I believe, to show that Macbeth sees being king much as a child playing dress-up does. He wants the crown, the title; he wants what is not rightfully his. In Act V we see what an utter mess Macbeth has made of his destiny: 'that which should accompany old age, / As honour, love, obedience, troops of friends, / I must not look to have; but in their stead, / Curses, not loud but deep, mouth-honour, breath, / Which the poor heart would fain deny and dare not.' His wife kills herself, for even she is disgusted by Macbeth's increasingly appalling actions. No one is loyal to him, and no one loves him. Macbeth's ignominious death is fitting. His decapitation by Macduff brings a sense of poetic justice. Once Malcolm is restored to the throne, Scotland will have a true king once again, whereas Macbeth will be remembered as a 'dead butcher'.

In conclusion, the theme of kingship is central to *Macbeth*. Many of the truths of leadership brought out in the play are still relevant today. We still see the damage caused when evil people have power, such as Hitler or Mugabe. We no longer believe in a God-given right to govern, which puts the onus on all of us to choose our leaders carefully. It was also interesting to learn about the monarchy and hereditary inheritance. Even when Britain's Prince William married Kate Middleton, she was repeatedly referred to as a 'commoner'! These contemporary references show once again how relevant Shakespeare continues to be, especially regarding the theme of kingship.

SAMPLE ESSAY 3

Write an essay in which you discuss the use of Imagery and Symbolism in Macbeth. *Support your answer with reference to the play.*

'Piece out our imperfections with your thought …
Think, when we talk of horses, that you see them …'
(Henry V)

The use of imagery in *Macbeth* is simply astonishing. Every line of this evocative play conjures up vivid images. This was a deliberate technique that Shakespeare used to compensate for the lack of props, scenery, etc. in the theatre of his day. In the pared-back setting of the Globe Theatre, audiences would simply imagine for themselves all that was necessary to make their viewing of this play a sensuous experience. There are many different types of imagery in *Macbeth*. The main ones are clothing imagery, storm imagery, bloody and violent imagery, and animal imagery. There is also much symbolism, for example 'the golden round'. The characters themselves may become symbols. Duncan is a symbol of goodness, whereas the Witches symbolise evil. Or the dagger: first clean then bloody, it also symbolises Macbeth's ability to be both good and evil.

In Shakespeare's day, clothing was expensive and hard to procure. Clothing proclaimed one's status. A simple glance at an outfit was often enough to assess a person's social status. Shakespeare was fond of using clothing imagery in all his plays. In *King Lear*, no one recognises Edgar when he disguises himself as a beggar. In *Othello*, a simple piece of linen convinces Othello of his wife's infidelity. In *Hamlet*, the title character's madness is symbolised by his sagging stockings and unlaced doublet. But it is in *Macbeth* that clothing becomes powerfully suggestive. Macbeth's view of being king is a fundamentally childish one. He covets the 'golden round' but has no idea of what it takes to be king. 'Now does he feel his title / Hang loose about him, like a giant's robe / Upon a dwarfish thief.' This speech by Angus so accurately sums up Macbeth's character, for he simply is not man enough to fill Duncan's shoes. Macduff had anticipated this earlier in the play, when he commented: 'Lest our old robes sit easier than our new!'

The clothing imagery in *Macbeth* serves two purposes, then. It creates vivid images and it shows how appearances can be deceptive. Macbeth can only ever steal the superficial trappings of being king – the crown and the clothing – but these do not make him king. I think Shakespeare was probably commenting on his society and how the rich and powerful could get away with anything. What really matters is having a good character and being thought well of. Ironically, Macbeth articulates this most clearly: 'I have bought / Golden opinions from all sorts of people, / Which would be worn now in their newest gloss, / Not cast aside so soon.' Clothing or the lack of it can also reveal the truth about a person. We see this when Lady Macbeth finally shows her true self in Act V, Scene I, when she is wearing only a nightgown. We realise that her earlier dress was a disguise to hide the vulnerable person on the inside. Stripped of her crown and queen's clothing, she is finally revealed to us.

The storm imagery in the play is used to create an ominous, foreboding atmosphere. Shakespeare's audience would have interacted with the elements in a way that a contemporary audience does not. So the description of the awful storm on the night of Duncan's murder would have had them shivering in the draughty theatre. '[T]his sore night / Hath trifled former knowings.' Even more alarming is the fact that it is dark when it should be light. Just as the Witches said that 'Fair is foul', the storm imagery is also symbolic. Nature is in revolt against Macbeth's unnatural reign. Light represents Duncan, night symbolises Macbeth. Therefore it cannot be light even in the day, because Macbeth's evil has condemned all to darkness.

Macbeth has been described as a play steeped in blood and gore, and this is undoubtedly true. The violence in this play is so prolific and so shocking that it is absolutely revolting. This I believe was Shakespeare's intention. The very first mention of Macbeth allies him with violence and death: 'he unseam'd him from the nave to the chaps / And fix'd his head upon our battlements'. This is a disturbingly graphic image, as is the one of Macbeth slicing his way through enemy lines: 'carved out his passage'. His wife's use of violent imagery is somehow worse, perverting the sacred bond of mother and child: 'I would … / Have pluck'd my nipple from his boneless gums / And dash'd the brains out'. I have never encountered such a horrific image!

All of the murders are described graphically. Macbeth's bloodied hands after Duncan's murder are symbolic as well as visual: 'Will all great Neptune's ocean wash this blood / Clean from my hand? No, this my hand will rather / The multitudinous seas incarnadine / Making the green one red.' Similarly, Banquo's violent passing is related to us explicitly – 'twenty trenched gashes on his head' – as is the appearance of his ghost: 'never shake / Thy gory locks at me'. I saw a version where the actor had been smothered with blood, which had crusted over his costume – stomach-churning but effective!

Blood imagery is also used to show how Macbeth feels that he has no choice but to continue on his bloody path: 'I am in blood / Stepp'd in so far that … / Returning were as tedious as go o'er.' Blood is also a key ingredient in the Witches' hideous potion; baboon's blood and the blood of a sow that has eaten her entire litter! Blood becomes a symbol of guilt, too. When we last see Lady Macbeth, she is desperately trying to wash her guilt away: 'Out, damned spot! Out, I say!' Lady Macbeth also mentions Duncan's blood: 'Yet who would have thought the old man to have had so much blood in him?' Yet it is the very absence of blood in this scene that makes it so effective. It is real to Lady Macbeth, and to us, because it represents her guilt and, in the end, her remorse.

Shakespeare was always fond of using animal imagery, and most of the animals mentioned in *Macbeth* have ominous connotations. Rooks, owls and hawks are mentioned, as is the bird which symbolises death: 'The raven himself is hoarse / That croaks the fatal entrance of Duncan / Under my battlements.' The hired assassins are compared to wild dogs or curs. Duncan's horses weirdly eat one another. The image of these sensitive creatures behaving thus is symbolic of the chaos created by Macbeth's reign.

The Witches throw all sorts of gruesome creatures into their cauldron: toads, newts, snakes, bats, worms, sharks, goats – even tigers. This undoubtedly helped created the sinister atmosphere of the 'cauldron scene'. However, my favourite example of animal imagery is in Act V, Scene VII: 'They have tied me to a stake; I cannot fly, / But bear-like I must fight the course.' The image of the once mighty bear, tied to a stake and lashing out blindly, although he knows he cannot reach anyone, is a perfect image for Macbeth.

There are many other kinds of imagery evident in *Macbeth*, and these images are often symbolic; take, for example, the proliferation of disease imagery. 'It weeps, it bleeds, and each new day a gash / Is added to her wounds,' is intended to picture Scotland sickening under Macbeth's reign. The country is an open sore which needs to be purged, meaning the rightful heir must be restored. Diseases and wounds, then, are a symbol of the inherent immorality of Macbeth being king. The original audience, often plagued with lice, fleas, sores and general ailments, would certainly have responded to this with empathy!

In conclusion, as I have demonstrated throughout my essay, imagery and symbolism played a huge role in *Macbeth*. Shakespeare has an innate ability to use images and symbols that are deceptively simple, like blood, for example. We all have a visceral reaction to this most vital of substances, and Shakespeare uses this to impress upon us the horror visited upon Scotland during Macbeth's reign.

SAMPLE ESSAY 5

'Lady Macbeth is not a monster. She is a loyal, if misguided wife, not without tenderness and not without conscience.'
Discuss this view of Lady Macbeth, referring to the play in support of your answer.

I would wholeheartedly agree with this statement. There is no doubt in my mind that, despite our first impressions of her, Lady Macbeth is not a monster, and I think her nervous collapse in Act V is ample proof of this. I also agree that she is completely loyal to her husband, even if that loyalty is the catalyst for so much death and destruction. Her tenderness is shown by this loyalty, and by the dramatic close of this play, her tortured conscience cannot be in doubt. Unbelievably, Lady Macbeth is only present in nine scenes of the play and yet in many ways her complicated character is even more compelling than that of her husband.

Our first introduction to Lady Macbeth comes in Act I, Scene V, when she reads Macbeth's letter to her aloud. This scene is incredibly tense and dramatic. Lady Macbeth seems to be unbelievably vicious and determined that her husband will become king no matter what: 'The raven himself is hoarse / That croaks the fatal entrance of Duncan under my battlements.' That a woman could have been so ruthless would have been utterly shocking to a contemporary audience. She knows that she will have to push Macbeth into committing murder and wishes that she were not a woman so that she could do it herself. She seems to see her sex as a handicap and asks the dark spirits to 'unsex' her, which hardly seems necessary to the audience as she seems so cold and ruthless already. A constant feature of Lady Macbeth is how she uses language to convince Macbeth, and us, that she is as unyielding as any man. She also echoes the Witches in her apparent communion with dark powers: 'Hie thee hither, / That I may pour my spirits in thine ear, / And chastise with the valour of my tongue / All that impedes thee from the golden round, / Which fate and metaphysical aid doth seem / To have thee crown'd withal.'

Macbeth's letter is the catalyst that spurs Lady Macbeth into action. But why does he write the letter, to be delivered by a messenger, when he is home himself only moments later? I believe Macbeth knew his wife would not let him rest until he was king. Lady Macbeth obviously knew of her husband's ambition and seems to feel that he will never be happy until he becomes king, through fair means or foul. Lady Macbeth never once expresses a desire to be queen. We can thus assume that this was not her primary motivation for plotting against Duncan, and that what she did, however terrible, was out of a misguided loyalty to Macbeth.

There is no doubt that the couple are close, and they are presented as being deeply in love. Macbeth refers to Lady Macbeth as his 'partner in greatness'. He seems to be in absolute awe of her. He has shared his most shameful desires with her, after all, and she has supported him without question. The main reason for their close bond is the secret ambition they share. There is also no doubt that Lady Macbeth manipulates her husband with ease. When he hesitates, she repeatedly questions his manliness until he feels that the murder is no longer a choice but a necessity: 'What beast was't, then, / That made you break this enterprise to me? / When you durst do it, then you were a man, / And, to be more than what you were, you would / Be so much more the man.' Only an incredibly insecure person would feel that he had to commit murder to prove his manhood, so while Lady Macbeth certainly plays a part in her husband's decline, the overall responsibility is undoubtedly his.

The events surrounding the murder of Duncan are what condemn Lady Macbeth, but also what redeem her. While she orchestrates the murder scene (laying out daggers in readiness and drugging the Grooms), she also has to drink to give herself courage: 'That which hath made them drunk hath made me bold'. Crucially, she cannot bring herself to kill Duncan, giving the excuse that 'Had he not resembled / My father as he slept I had done 't.' This shows her tender side. However, when a distraught and disorientated Macbeth emerges in horror from Duncan's chamber, Lady Macbeth makes herself further culpable by returning the daggers, smearing the Grooms' faces with blood and, most significantly, calming her husband down. Had she not used her persuasion to challenge her husband's broken demeanour – 'My hands are of your colour, but I shame / To wear a heart so white' – he would have been caught and punished immediately. So, not only does she have Duncan's blood on her hands, literally and metaphorically, indirectly Lady Macbeth is also responsible for the other murders which ensue, a fact she acknowledges before her suicide.

When we next meet Lady Macbeth and her husband (after Macduff has discovered Duncan's body), their roles seem to have been reversed. Macbeth lies brilliantly and seems entirely self-contained. Lady Macbeth, on the other hand, faints, and while some would argue that this is a clever tactic to distract attention from Macbeth, who has made a tactical error in killing the Grooms, I would say that she faints in genuine horror at the changed man her husband has become in such a short space of time. This view is certainly backed up by her changed behaviour throughout the rest of the play.

Macbeth's first action as king is to hire assassins to kill his best friend and comrade, Banquo, whom he believes is a challenge to his rule. Lady Macbeth had no involvement in this murder: 'Be innocent of the knowledge, dearest chuck, / Till thou applaud the deed.' Indeed, Lady Macbeth tries to persuade her husband to be satisfied with what he has achieved: ''Tis safer to be that which we destroy / Than by destruction dwell in doubtful joy.' When Macbeth's guilty conscience makes him believe he sees Banquo's bloody Ghost at the banquet, Lady Macbeth loyally tries to cover for her husband. But her attempts to do so seem desperate and weak. She is very different in this third act from the monster of Act I, and Act II is the vital link in making her character credible despite this. In Act IV she is entirely absent, while her husband's deeds grow ever more degenerate.

The first scene of Act V is utterly shocking in its depiction of Lady Macbeth. She is a pathetically vulnerable figure sleepwalking through the castle, desperately trying to wash away an invisible bloodstain: 'Out, damned spot!' This scene has an important dramatic function. Everything in it links with previous scenes; it shows that crime never pays; and it is a powerful visual spectacle, too. The sight of a lady in a nightgown, which would have been very risqué in Shakespeare's day, portrays vulnerability very intensely. Lady Macbeth simply cannot cope with the extent of her guilt. It is all-consuming and relentless. The fact that she (apparently) kills herself signals her total inability to deal with the legacy of her and her husband's crimes but also redeems her in the eyes of the audience: 'What, will these hands ne'er be clean?'

In conclusion, as I have demonstrated throughout my essay, I believe that the statement that 'Lady Macbeth is not a monster. She is a loyal, if misguided wife, not without tenderness and not without conscience' is completely true. I found Lady Macbeth's character to be absolutely intriguing throughout my study of the play. At first I thought she was a monster, especially when she said, 'I have given suck and know / How tender 'tis to love the babe that milks me; / I would, while it was smiling in my face / .... dash'd the brains out, had I so sworn as you / Have done to this.' But Shakespeare breaks her down brilliantly, stage by stage, so that her eventual disintegration into a guilt-ridden suicide is utterly believable. I thought Francesca Annis portrayed Lady Macbeth brilliantly in Roman Polanski's version of *Macbeth*. Although she seemed fierce at first, there was always an underlying softness. Even when chiding her husband for taking the daggers from Duncan's chamber, for example, her voice was shaking slightly, hinting at the vulnerability and tenderness that lay underneath, even if she disguised it well. Shakespeare intended this play to be performed on stage, and I think it is in actual performances that the brilliance of Lady Macbeth's character, with all its subtle nuances, is best seen.

PAST LEAVING CERT EXAM QUESTIONS ON MACBETH

(2003)
'We feel very little pity for the central characters of Macbeth and Lady Macbeth in Shakespeare's play.' To what extent would you agree with the above view? Support your answer by reference to the play.

(2003)
'In *Macbeth*, Shakespeare presents us with a powerful vision of evil.' Write your response to the above statement. Textual support may include reference to a particular performance of the play you have seen.

(2004)
'Shakespeare's *Macbeth* invites us to look into the world of a man driven on by ruthless ambition and tortured by regret.' Write a response to this view of the play, *Macbeth*, supporting the points you make by reference to the text.

(2004)
'The play, *Macbeth*, has many scenes of compelling drama.' Choose one scene that you found compelling and say why you found it to be so. Support your answer by reference to the play.

(2007)

'The relationship between Macbeth and Lady Macbeth undergoes significant change during the course of the play.' Discuss this statement, supporting your answer with the aid of suitable reference to the text.

(2007)

'Essentially the play *Macbeth* is about power, its use and abuse.' Discuss this view of the play, supporting your answer with the aid of suitable reference to the text.

(2009)

'Macbeth's murder of Duncan has horrible consequences both for Macbeth himself and for Scotland.' Write a response to this statement. You should refer to the play in your answer.

(2009)

'*Macbeth* has all the ingredients of compelling drama.' Write a response to this statement, commenting on one or more of the ingredients that, in your opinion, make *Macbeth* a compelling drama.

CLASSROOM ACTIVITIES AND GROUP WORK

The Cauldron Game:
Write out each ingredient five times on slips of paper and place in a 'cauldron' (any container will do). Let each student pick one ingredient, for example 'eye of newt' (double up if necessary). If your ingredient is pulled from the cauldron, you get a point. The first to get five points is the winner.

The Courtroom Game:
The premise of this game is that there is just one place left in hell, and so, by default, either Lady Macbeth or Macbeth is getting into heaven. Pick two students to play Lady Macbeth and Macbeth, and one student to play God. Arrange the class as a courtroom. Both characters can have their own team of lawyers, and the rest of the class can be the witnesses and the jury. Macbeth's lawyers can cross-examine Lady Macbeth, and Lady Macbeth's lawyers can cross-examine Macbeth. Witnesses can be called (such as Banquo). Evidence can be taken from the text. The jury can decide who is worse: Macbeth for killing Duncan or Lady Macbeth for pushing him into it.

Imagery Group Work:
Divide the class into four groups (clothing, animal, blood, storm), and let each group find five examples of imagery.

Apparitions:
Draw the four Apparitions from Act IV, Scene I.

The author and publisher wish to thank the Utah Shakespeare Festival, Cedar City, Utah, USA, for permission to reproduce photographs of their various productions of *Macbeth* in this book

Photographer: Karl Hugh, © Utah Shakespeare Festival

Cast:

The Witches	PAGE 16	*(l-r)* Chelsea Steverson, Lillian Castillo, Monica Lopez (2010)
	PAGE 135	Pat Sibley (2004)
	PAGE 157	*(l-r)* Misty Cotton, Pat Sibley, Afton Quast (2004)
	PAGE 205	*(l-r)* Todd Zimbleman, Jennifer Whipple, Kelly Marie Hennessey (2011)
Macbeth	PAGE 47	Grant Goodman (2010)
	PAGE 123	Henry Woronicz (2004)
Lady Macbeth	PAGE 47	Kymberly Mellen (2010)
	PAGE 86	Carole Healey (2004)
Banquo	PAGE 93	Don Burroughs (2010)
Macduff	PAGE 155	Michael Brusasco (2010)
Lady Macduff	PAGE 141	Stephanie Erb (2004)
	PAGE 159	Caroline Crocker (2010)
Malcolm	PAGE 155	Quinn Mattfeld (2010)
Doctor	PAGE 167	Ron Thomas (2010)
Gentlewoman	PAGE 167	Kymberly Mellen (2010)

Other photograph:

PAGE 56   *Stacy Ross and Jud Williford – California Shakespeare Theatre (2010)* © Kevin Byrne

Actors featured in illustrations:

PAGE 51   Christopher Carlos and Christina Vela – *Kitchen Dog Theater (2011)*
PAGE 61   CJ Wilson – *Berkshire Theatre Festival (2010)*
PAGE 81   Helen Rynne – *The Long Overdue Theatre Company (2009)*
PAGE 174   Jonathan Holtzman – *American Shakespeare Center (2010)*